The Lifestyle
Salon Owner

The Lifestyle
Salon Owner

Richard McCabe

Published by www.lulu.com

THE LIFESTYLE SALON OWNER

ISBN 978-0-244-07608-5

Contents

Acknowledgements

Writing a book on my life's work was the easy part, the actual journey was thrilling, nervous, exciting, scary and in some parts unimaginable hard work!

This book is the outcome of many people and situations that have come my way, and today I would like to publicly thank them all, and my apologies if I have forgotten anyone.

To my parents without whom my salon life would not have started, thank you for lending me some of the money to kick start me off.

To my friends Dale, Stef, Toni and Phil who gave up their time to help build my salon literally from the ground up.

To my first staff members in the UK Kelly, Sammy, Kayleigh, Chrissy and of course Sandra who gave me 8 loyal years, helping me take my first salon Samson's to great heights.

Then moving to Australia to start a new adventure and without the help of Lin and Vic my Mother and Father in law, taking us in under their wings and helping us build our new foundations in Gods Country.

To my salon staff at Retreat Hairdressing which was full of great loyal staff and I would never be here today if it wasn't for such a bunch of passionate motivated staff. They helped make Retreat the salon it was,

Amanda, Tamiya, Bec, Tamara, Danny, Lauren, Keesha and Beth I thank you all for your commitment to the cause and your loyalty to me.

To my mentors Murray Slatter, Nergish Wadia Austin, Beatrice Dautzenberg, and Taki Moore for helping and encouraging me to be better at what I do.

To my fellow coaches Nicole McDonell and Julie Lee thank you for your support and guidance in the lonely world of coaching.

To my children Charlie, Brett and Kurtis, for never complaining about me working long hours and missing school plays.

And last but not least, my wife Mandy, my rock, for backing me when no one else would, for pulling me back when I go off track, for being there right at the beginning where it all started when the hard work was happening and for being the unsung hero in the background and no one sees what you do, just getting the right stuff done.

Without you and your support none of this could have ever been accomplished. Thank you for painstakingly deciphering my thoughts and words and carefully constructing them into this book for everyone to read, this book would never have been written without you.

Without these people this book would never have been written, I thank you all.

Introduction

They laughed when I became a hairdresser but stopped the day I moved house to the most expensive suburb in my town. But that's not where it all started...

I remember my first day owning and opening my very first salon, I was excited, I was giddy, I couldn't wait to open the doors, I thought it was going to be so easy. I thought the clients would come in droves and they would love me, because I was really good at hairdressing. I always found it easy to build a full clientele, so it wouldn't be long before the salon would be full to the brim, I'd be making loads of money, living in a nice big house and driving a big flash car and everyone knowing that I'd made a success of it, that I was a success! It wasn't long before the reality hit home and my excitement and dream were a distant memory.

If you are anything like me as a salon owner, I thought all it took to make my salon a success was to be good at what I did, and clients would fall in love with me, they'd tell all their friends and my salon would be fully booked in 12 months. Many, many years ago that may have been the case, but times have changed, and just being good at what you do is not enough anymore.

Every salon owner I have ever met has the capability to grow their salon to give them the perfect lifestyle that they desire, which is astonishing really considering how they became a business owner in the first place. Some had bad bosses and they didn't want to be treated that way anymore, others left their previous employment due to the fact that they thought they could run a salon better, they wanted to look after their clients better or they were mistreated by their boss and they thought when I get a salon of my own it's going to be different. I will treat my staff 10 times better than I've been treated. I will pay my staff more money, give them respect, time off when they ask, and I will train them to be the best they can be. I left my boss because he was mean with money and mean in his demeanour, I promised myself that I would be different when I employed staff.

The problem is, this is never how it is! We don't know the other side of what's affecting the decisions of our bosses, why it is that they are mean, grumpy and tight with their money. But when we opened our salon we soon realised why our boss was the way he was. He was either struggling with the bills or struggling to pay the wages or struggling to pay tax, juggling and struggling with the demands of staff calling in sick and the stress would get to him and hence he would take it out on (me or you).

I remember only too well myself doing exactly the same thing that my boss used to do to me and this was not where I wanted to be, I promised myself that I would not become the same as him, but I was and I hated myself for it. I'm not sure whether you are at this stage right now?

I guess it's not our fault, as understandable as it is because we lack direction and skill in a subject that we don't like and really have no interest in, because most people became hairdressers or beauticians and eventually salon owners because we were good with people and with our hands. We never liked school much, we didn't like maths, we loved people though, we loved the socialising, we were social butterflies. But when it came to the business side of things, the nitty gritty of organising structures we didn't like that so much. So we revert to what we know and that's our old bosses way, but what used to work back in the day does not work today and that's a huge problem. We also don't know business, numbers and systems, we don't like confrontations and we certainly don't want to tell our friends off, we just want to do hair or beauty, that's our forte, we're bloody good at it and it's fun.

The world in which we used to attract clients has changed so much, gone are the days of Yellow Pages and newspaper ads (the reason we liked these was because someone else did all the work for us, they would design the ad and everything), leaving us to concentrate on what we loved to do, hairdressing. But in the evolving times and the invention of Facebook, social media and Google the client has become savvier than ever before. They are even checking us out online before they visit us. We have to be so much more perfect than ever before.

NOTE: Most hair and beauty people are social butterflies and that means we should be kings and queens of social media, it's not as hard as you think, we should be owning our space on these platforms.

As far back as I remember my coach in the UK told me that a salon filled with average workers that deliver remarkable service will out perform a salon filled with super stars (who wants to work in a salon with superstars, imagine the ego's flying around in there)!

The times have changed and being good at your trade is not enough, so why do salon owners find it so difficult to make their salons successful? With 80% of salon owners crashing and burning within 5 years, the odds are stacked against you. I don't believe they were all bad at what they did, what they were bad at was attracting clients and keeping them. You see the clients have changed, they are savvier than ever and are wanting more.

Many salon owners are good at what they do, they are trained well and deliver above average results but you need to be different from the rest. You need to set your salon apart in order to make your salon successful; clients need to see you are different.

The 3 ways to grow any business

With only 3 ways to grow any business, why do so many salon owners get this so wrong, not only to get their salons to survive but to thrive?

The only 3 ways to grow your business:

1. Get more bums on seats (more clients),
2. Get the bums on seats to visit more often (to get the clients to come and visit you more regularly)
3. Get bums on seats to spend more (to get your clients average bill up),

If it's as simple as only doing 3 things to get your salon busy then why don't we do it, why do we struggle so much and why has no one ever said before, that it's only 3 things we need to spend our time on?

It's not your fault, no-one has ever shown you how to do it. You spend most of your days putting fires out and working harder to try and make more money. But that way is old fashioned and the new way is simpler than you think. After reading this book you will have mastered the 3 ways to grow your business and will be closer to getting a great lifestyle from your salon. But first let's take stock of where you are now and this will determine what you need to do next.

The 3 types of salon owner

As a business coach I have observed hundreds and thousands of salon owners around the world and at any given time they are at one of three stages in their salon owners journey. Knowing where your salon sits will help you concentrate on what you should be working on next to take your salon to the next level.

The 3 types of salon owners:

Start Up Zone: The **Start Up Zone** is usually year 1 or year 2. It's the passion that is driving the salon growth and you're so excited, you don't even want to pay yourself a wage, you just want to survive and you're happy with that and you're happy to work 70 hours a week with little money and the passion is really alive. Clients love you and most clients are referring you like crazy. In fact you get so busy you need to employ 1 or 2 staff members and life is great. The salon is buzzing and you're proud as punch that the salon is in fact doing far better than you could ever imagine.

War Zone: You enter the **war zone** naturally as your salon grows. We call it the **war zone** as most salon owners move into this zone and never get out of it. You know you are in the **war zone** if you are scared to discipline your staff incase they leave and take their clients with them;

you attract clients that you shouldn't do just because you become desperate and need the money. It's like a battle field as salons fight over clients and staff, the only way you know how to react is with money, either offering discounts to attract clients, and offering more money to attract staff. With so many salons doing this every salon owner reacts by doing it more and more. Bigger discounts to attract the clients, and offer more money to attract and keep the staff. This has a massive effect on the salons profits and it soon becomes apparent to you, the salon owner, that things are very tight on the financial front, the bills are starting to pile up to a really scary amount and you're wondering how on earth you're going to be able to pay them. The bills start to come fast and furious and takings take a nose dive, the staff lose their passion and morale and then the reality really hits home. The staff are NOT pulling their weight (it's not their fault, doing cheap work, with clients they don't like, this is not what they wanted when they became a hairdresser or beautician). You get angry with them and start to pass the blame onto them.

With the added pressure of staff today being more demanding and not wanting to work late nights, nor wanting to work weekends, and of course wanting more money, they too feel that they could do a better job than you and they soon feel that owning a salon themselves is a good idea, once that seed is set, the battle is lost. That results in a lot of smaller salons opening in your town that are fighting for the same clients as you.

It's a **war zone** out there!

You cannot take anymore as your passion is slowly slipping away and everything starts to annoy you, the pressure is on and you react to every no show, every sick day that the staff have and before you know it, you have become your old boss, stressed and desperate. You will know you are in this zone if you are working long hours, the busiest person in the salon and may even pay yourself less than your staff. The bills rise so big that you either have to use your own private money to keep the salon afloat or put your bills and taxes on credit and that is the first stage of the slippery slope to closing your salons door.

If that's you at the moment just breathe a little, this book will help you build the steps needed to take your salon out of this **war zone** and into the **lifestyle zone**. You will need to learn some simple business skills. The 3 steps of growing a business to get your salon out of this depressing zone. If you get to learn these simple formulas, then you will move into what we call the **lifestyle zone**. And that's when life really becomes interesting.

Lifestyle Zone: The **lifestyle zone** is all about the salon being a destination and not you. You tend to work less hours on the salon floor and spend more of your working day driving the business to be better, you get paid an awful lot more money for the amount of work you do. In fact for most salon owners in this zone they pay themselves what they want. It means that you've got more control, the business isn't about you anymore, the business is about the salon and we call that the **lifestyle zone** because that's usually where you start living the lifestyle that you wanted when you first opened your own salon all those years ago. You can take holidays when you like and your staff know that you are there to drive the business and make them better at what they do.

When you have systems in place and money in your bank account it's amazing how most of your troubles disappear. Your staff are all booked out and you have time to work the hours you want. You have the time to get to learn new techniques that grow your salon faster, you get time off with your family and the salon staff are proud, because they have great high paying clients and you pay them a decent wage.

In the **lifestyle zone** you have more money, more purpose and more freedom.

Without systems it's near impossible to get your salon into the **lifestyle zone.** Your salon needs systems as your business grows because it gets so chaotic, the more clients and staff you have, the more problems that can, and nearly always do, arise.

You may have noticed that it's harder to find clients and even harder to find staff in todays busy world. In fact we are bombarded with 5,000 ads/branding messages per day, we would have to see one every 11.52 seconds so our brain just switches off from them all. So all of your posts, adverts and messages that you are doing now are not getting seen, the problem is what used to work in the old days doesn't work anymore. All you had to do in the old days was be good at your trade, get loyal clients to come to you, be really good at what you do and that was it, the business would grow organically on its own. You would place an advert for staff and you would get lots of people apply for the position and you could be choosey. Today you need to drive that message home and that takes time and skill.

But the new way brings its own problems, as salon owners just don't know how to do this. They think it's about putting an ad on Facebook and clients will come flocking in. Remember Facebook and other social media outlets are just that SOCIAL, people go there to be social not to be sold to. You and I should do well on these platforms as we are social butterflies, the problem is we are impatient and want results today and that is what's turning clients away from your salon forever. But salons that embrace the new way, put time and effort into building their foundations will grow faster and enter the **lifestyle zone** as other salon owners fight over the scraps. In todays world staff and clients demand more, they will not accept second best any more and will leave these salons in their droves to go to other salons that offer more of what they desire.

Why Me Why Now

I left school with very limited education and started my hairdressing apprenticeship at the age of 16. I was the most unmotivated person you could imagine (I wouldn't have employed me, but my first boss saw something in me that I didn't know I had). I worked at a very busy and demanding town centre salon until I reached my 2nd year and the salon was sold and I moved my apprenticeship to a small suburban salon to finish my trade. Learning at the two different types of salon built my skills up fast. The one thing I did notice was employer 1, the town centre salon owner drove a Porsche, and employer 2 drove a Jaguar. I knew there was money to be made in hairdressing but just not as an employee so I knew I had to go out on my own.

I, of course, just like you thought I knew better than my boss. I thought I was the bees knees and all the clients loved me, and I thought he would close down when I left. I really thought I was that good (lol he's still open today). I started my very first business, as a mobile hairdresser (I thought all the clients would leave the salon and come to me, they didn't), I loved the hours, the buzz and of course the money.

The problem was that I had no self control and the money soon disappeared and the bills piled up. I quickly realised that mobile hairdressing had its limitations and I would always have to work all the hours for a small wage. With a wife and 3 children I needed more. I wanted more out of life, I wanted the nice house and the nice car and the holidays overseas.

So I decided to set up my first salon, excited and scared (so scared I took on a business partner to help me, it soon collapsed 1 week in, and left me broke, but that's another story for another day). I was eager to open the doors and start to earn my fortune, this was it, my very own hair salon.

I still remember my very first client walking in at 2.00pm saying,"I bet I'm your first client?", I told him no he wasn't and did the best hair cut ever on him. He was still a clients 5 years on and I did eventually come clean and tell him he was correct, he was my first ever client.

The salon grew fast, people liked me and every day seemed busy, I loved the buzz of a pumping salon, I still do today. I employed staff and they too got busy, this salon owner malarky was easy, I was dreaming of the house I was going to buy and my new car parked in the double garage.

Then the growth just stopped, I didn't know why at the time, it just stopped, I wasn't too bothered as we were busy but year after year our growth just seemed minimal. But then it hit me straight between the eyes, I was making money, lots of it, but the bigger my salon became the bigger and faster the bills came in.

It felt like I was working hard for not much in return. At the end of every financial year my accountant would say, "What a good year you have had", but I had nothing in the bank to show for it, in fact it was getter harder and harder to stay ahead of the bills, how could this be so?

I think this is when the cracks started to appear and I started noticing that my staff were turning up late just 5 minutes or so, and some staff were asking for pay rises, I even heard one staff member say to another, in the back room, "We are paying Richards mortgage, we're fools". At one stage I think some staff were stealing money and products from me, I even felt that some clients were not returning, and the salon numbers dropped fast. Had this been going on for a while? Had I only just woken up to the fact that my salon was not as good as I thought it was? I will never know the real answer to what was really going on behind my back in the salon, but what I did next was so typical of salon owners like me, I see this so many times with my coaching clients.

I decided the best way to deal with this was to ignore it and it will go away. I didn't know what else to do, I was a salon owner that just knew how to do great hairdressing, that's all I knew, I didn't know anything about business at all. I was scared to reprimand the staff because when I did they wouldn't turn up for work, or they would exclude me from their circle, I was scared that they would leave and I would lose more clients, This resulted in my bills starting to get to a place where I was scared that if a staff member left and took clients I wouldn't be able to afford my bills and I ended up in what I called 'groundhog day' where every day was pain, every day was juggling bills, every day it just seemed I was 1 step away from really closing my doors, 1 step away from failure.

To the outside world I had a really successful salon but no one else knew behind the scenes that I was struggling, it was feast or famine. I seemed to have a good month and a bad month, and a good month and a bad month and at the end of the year I had nothing to show for the fact that I was a business owner, all I really had was a job and the problem with this job was the boss didn't know what he was doing, and that was me!

I remember this one year taking my eye right off the ball and my wife saying to me, "We don't have enough money to pay the tax bill", and we had to make that awkward phone call to the tax office to say, "Can we put our tax on the never, never". That was the start of our failure, because we're struggling to pay the bills at the moment, it just put added pressure on us and slowly took us deeper and deeper into debt. I know from my own mistakes it's all too easy to take your eye off the ball as a salon owner as your business grows, because the bills are massive and it will cripple you if you have a bad month or a staff member walks out.

I don't know about you but I remember waking up in the middle of the night with fear about not being able to pay the bills, fear of paying the wages. I became a master of juggling all my money, cash flow was non existent, and I was stealing from Peter to pay Paul on a daily basis. I even managed to convince anyone who asked "How's the salon doing?", and I would say, "It's doing great, we are so busy", but I was dying inside. l had already decided the best way to try and fix this problem was for me to work 6 days a week, sometimes 7, and work harder and harder and longer and longer hours and just cram more clients in with me, as I knew they loved me; to try and fix this problem. The only problem was that I made my salon so dependent on me I couldn't take time off ever, no holidays, even having to work when I was really sick, but the harder I worked in the salon and the more clients I did I just never seemed to make enough money.

I seemed to be the only person working that hard in the salon, I was the busy fool! The clients all wanted me and I was happy because every client I did I thought I was paying off my bills faster. I had no family time, work revolved completely around my business. I had no systems in place at all. The passion, my passion that was driving the salon was slowly disappearing from me, and that is bad, as I was the only passionate person in the salon.

It took me to breaking point before I realised that I must be the problem, I must be doing something wrong. It was me all along.

I decided that I didn't want a salon like this, I would rather work for someone. So I decided to give it one last try, I drew my line in the sand and went that's enough I can't do this anymore. It's so hard I was one step away from losing my house, one step away from my kids moving school, one step away from not even being able to afford to pay for my food. Not that my salon wasn't doing well it's just that I had no control. I thought if I had one staff member leave me, I was gone, it's as simple as that. I was great at hairdressing that was for sure (all the clients I did loved me) So my downfall must be business, I didn't know anything about business, so I decided to learn everything I could about being a better business man.

I started simple with buying every leadership, business, marketing and financial books I could and I learnt how to read them and take action on what I learned.

I went to every seminar I could find, with every so called expert in their field, I learnt lots and brought that back to the salon and practiced and practiced.

I employed a business coach (very expensive in those days) and learnt some quick ways to condense everything I had learned to get results fast.

Then one day it all clicked into place, I realised that it was my journey that I was on and no one is going to stop me achieving this, this is my dream and my staff were either going to help me or they were going to hinder me and my role as a salon owner was to start taking steps towards my dream and see who was joining me. I told them my dream, I told them we're going to go on this journey, I told them that we were going to systemise the business so that we can all have more clients and all have more money and those who wanted to come with me and learn the new techniques and get there, they would get the spoils, and those that were lazy and enjoyed sitting in the backroom for 3 hours a day they would be left behind because it's their choice to come or to go. It was my way or the highway! I didn't need to decide or make the big decision to sack people who were not pulling their weight, the staff made that decision, it was out of my hands now. It was up to them if they wanted to help me achieve my dream or hinder me. My decision was to man up and act on their decision. I knew what I had to do.

My staff gave me resistance for sure, of course they did, some still wanted to come to work, sit around and watch me work all day to pay their wages. But for me it was an eye opener, I stayed strong and told myself that my staff had two choices, to follow me and help me make this work for the benefit of the salon, or they will be left behind, it was their decision and it wasn't up to me to make that choice. I was free at last.

Year after year we grew again, but it was different, it wasn't frantic, it was controlled. The staff were busier than me, and clients asked for them first. The salon ran smoothly when I wasn't there. They looked up to me, they knew my role was to grow the salon and grow them as people. I loved being a business man. I don't know what was the defining moment but the salon was a dream to own. It paid me lots of money, I had time off with my family.

Taking everything I had learnt over the years and figuring out what worked and what didn't I soon realised that it was much simpler than I thought. I could see clarity, I saw something that was so unique, so brilliant and so simple that changed my life forever.

I knew what I was about to build in my salon was a game changer, life changing systems that will get me to my dream, I knew I wanted a lifestyle salon, I knew I wanted to live in a certain suburb, I knew what school I wanted my kids to go to, I knew I wanted more freedom, more purpose and more money in life. I wanted to thrive not just survive.

So I went about systemising my business based on the 3 core elements, consisting of 9 simple steps, that grow businesses fast.

> **Attract** - Set my salon apart from other salons and attract clients at will, get more bums on seats.
> **Convert** - Get clients to become raving fans, get the clients to visit more often
> **Deliver** - Bring back the client experience, the 'wow factor' like they have never seen before, get the clients to spend more each and every visit.

Within 12 months of implementing the new strategies we broke it all down to 3 core elements, consisting of 9 simple steps. I learnt how to **attract** clients to my salon, in a different way from any other salon in town, so that clients chased me, not the other way around, me chasing them. I then learnt how to **convert** these clients to come in on my quiet days and come more often and the difference was thousands of dollars, no one else was doing this, and they're still not. We then realised if we **delivered** an absolutely remarkable result that was predictable every time the clients came in, then clients stayed an extra 2-3 years more than any other salons in town. **Attract, Convert, Deliver** grew my business to give me the lifestyle I dreamed of many years before.

Not all of the staff followed us and within 12 months we'd lost 2 or 3 staff members, gained 3 or 4 more new ones, but I was in control of one of the busiest salons in my town.

Fast forward another 15 years and I'm living in a whole new country, in Australia and have had multiple salons since and have used these 9 simple steps on every salon I've owned, they work impeccably well. I've been a salon owner for over 20 years and I have used these and tweaked them and honed my skills to keep them modern and relevant, and today I am going to share these skills with you in this book.

You will have the same power and the same knowledge that I had all those years ago, but without wasting time because they've been tried and tested.

You will have noticed that the world outside your salon has changed and will keep on changing. The savvy salon owner will learn to adapt, because the staff have changed and so have the clients. The salon owner that says the world needs to change to him is wrong and will be left behind.

In this changing world it seems clients and staff don't seem to be as loyal as they once were.

Hence why we are going through the biggest staff shortage worldwide as we speak. Salon owners can't find them or keep them, (as salon owners we have to take some of the blame here as we have turned so many staff off hair or beauty with our moaning or lack of business skills) staff are bored, they haven't got enough wages, they're passionless and they're demotivated, and that all comes from you the salon owner because you don't know business enough. You don't know how to attract clients to your salon to fill your staffs days, so that they can earn more money, in turn making you more money which you can then share with your team by giving you the opportunity to get them on the best training courses on the planet.

Believe it or not your staff want to belong to something bigger than them and their column, staff today want to do famous people like Jennifer Aniston or Kim Kardashians hair. They want their 15 minutes of fame.

Now you and I both know we can't give them Kim Kardashian or Jennifer Aniston's hair but we can give them their 15 minutes of fame. That could be in the form of a training course in New York or London or Paris or Las Vegas or Sydney. So they come home and share the stories of what they've learnt and where they have been with friends and family, that's their 15 minutes of fame.

Also you can get your colour company (since you spend a lot of money with them) to help you get your team onto shows working on stage, around the world, that's their 15 minutes of fame, that's their Kim Kardashian, and their Jennifer Aniston right there. It's up to you to deliver that. If you can get this right your staff will stay around for a long time, be loyal and make you lots of money in the process.

Imagine if you could pay your staff twice as much as every other salon in town, You also paid for them to go on a 2 week trip around the world to learn from the best of the best. They do shows on stage and felt confident in everything they do, their hairdressing or beauty friends are envious of them, other salon owners are envious too, do you think your next advert for staff would result in no one.applying? Do you think staff would ever leave you, where would they get that from at any other salon?

Then if that's the case imagine for just one moment that your salon was full, your staff didn't leave you they stayed around for a long time and they built up their clientele and they worked 4 days a week, they travelled the world doing shows and training, every staff member was doing 3 times their wage plus some more, you had money in the bank, your children went to the best school, you lived in a really good area, you could get your salon refitted out every 5 years and everybody knew you were having a big refit and there was excitement in the salon. You offered the best training in the world, you could have bigger premises if ever you wanted, you had the best of everything, the clients loved you and came and stayed forever (after all why would they leave, your staff are travelling the world, they too want their 15 minutes of fame as they tell their friends what their hairdresser or beautician has been doing). You had time to breathe, bills were never a problem again, that's a real **lifestyle salon** we're talking about here.

When this happens staff treat you like 'the go to salon'. You put an advert in the paper and they come in their droves because they want to work at your salon, and let's be honest who wouldn't. I'd want to work there, it's the salon that anyone and everyone wants to work for. You pay them the most, they have the most enjoyment in life, they live life to the fullest. We do life with these people, we owe it to them, they work hard for us, we owe it to them to give them a good life so they can buy good cars, good houses and travel the world. We're building lifelong friends here and we have the opportunity to change lives across the board.

That's where I want to take you on this journey in this book. I want to show you the simple steps it takes to get your salon into the **lifestyle zone**.

This book will breakdown the 9 simple steps that made my salon a **lifestyle salon**, this simple formula that I found when I got my true **lifestyle salon**.

I talked earlier on about there being only 3 ways to grow your business, **attract** more clients to your salon, **convert** them to come more often and **deliver** a remarkable service so that your average bill, retail and rebooks go up.

To sum up the 3 core foundational elements to grow your salon business:

Attract
Convert
Deliver

Each core element is made up of 3 simple steps.

These are the 9 simple steps that I used in my own salon business, and that I teach my **Lifestyle** salon clients. These strategies help us generate clients, convert clients into raving fans, and deliver remarkable results. That way I can help hundreds of salon owners all over the world to achieve the same kind of results I'd get if I was working with them one to one.

These are the nine strategies that drive a salon out of the War Zone and into the Lifestyle Zone

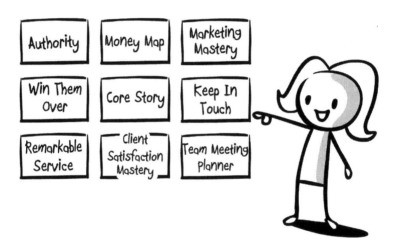

In **Part One,** we'll look at three strategies that make up the Attract formula of your salon business.

In **Strategy 1,** I'll show you how to build your **Salons Authority** as clients are more savvy these days and want to go to **'the salon expert'.** We'll work on your **'what to say'** and **'how often'** you need to put your message out to get noticed. As we all know adverts **DO NOT** work any more. We'll get you the new clients and money you're after.

In **Strategy 2**, we build you a clear path, a **'Money Map'** Model; with a goal to get you to 30% and higher takings this year. The key to how many clients you need, who they are and how do you find them. We want to get this up and running early so it will immediately impact your bottom line profit.

In **Strategy 3**, I'll show you how to focus on **Marketing Mastery...** where we focus not only on **'HOW'** to post to get you more clients, but also on making sure you have **'accountability systems'** to track that those posts and adverts get done correctly and consistently, which will maximise your salons growth. How to work out social media, to build a rhythm so you do it on your busiest day and your quietest day. You will never sit in front of a computer again and not know what to do and what to talk about.

In **Part Two**, we'll dive deeply into three strategies that help you convert clients into raving fans and fill up your quiet days.

In **Strategy 4**, I'll show you what to do when you have been seen and noticed by new clients, we need to **'Win Them Over'**. They will go and check you out; branding your salon is a MUST to get prospective clients to believe in your story. You'll have your Facebook page and website have a makeover that portrays your story and build your credibility too.

In **Strategy 5**, we will set to work on your **'Core Story'**. As you are aware old style marketing just doesn't cut it with the new savvy client, so we need to tell **'our story'**, **'our way'**. Story telling has been at the forefront of getting clients and customers for some years now. You will share your **'vision'**, your **'why'** and your **'knowledge'** on your current clients. This story will be the backbone of everything you do, getting staff and clients alike.

In **Strategy 6**, we will make you some easy money. One of the most overlooked opportunities for salon owners to increase their takings and make more money is hidden in their computer system. You will learn how to get clients to stay loyal to you and also learn the secrets to getting clients to visit more often. **This Keep In Touch Strategy** can increase takings by a whopping $50,000 in a year.

Part Three, focuses on the delivery side of your salon, learning how to make your salon the destination and NOT you.

In **Strategy 7**, You will learn one of the keys to getting your salon to earn **MORE** while you are working **LESS**, the **'Remarkable Service'**... you'll be able to grow your salon and increase your income, without adding any more hours to your day. This is about making the 'SALON' a destination, 'NOT YOU'. Getting your salon standards perfect and systemised is like multiplying you times 10 and NOT making YOU the busiest person in the salon, which will free up your time to run the salon you have always dreamed of.

In **Strategy 8**, I'll show you how to focus on **Client Satisfaction Mastery**... where we focus not only on **'HOW'** to do a great consultation, but also on making sure you have every step of the client journey mapped out. Which will maximise your retail and service sales!

In **Strategy 9**, Once we've plugged all the major leaks in your salon and decked you out with some of the best tools in the industry... you'll be ready to multiply your success and crank up your team's results. In our **'Team Meeting Planner'** not only will we determine the meeting rhythms you need to maximise accountability, but also we will make sure you have a detailed outline of the BIG picture (how much your salon is expected to grow this year) and portray this to the smaller picture (how you will get your team to do their part). The most important meetings are based on teaching your team about all that you will be learning in this course to keep them productive and on track. (Oh yeah, and learn the secret to get you to stop motivating them, and how to get your team to motivate themselves willingly!)

For the last 3 years I've been a **lifestyle salon coach** and have taught hundreds of salon owners all around the world how to use this system with online courses and live events.

These 9 simple steps are working in salons all around the world as we speak today. In your hands right now you have the power that I had to convert my salon into one of the highest earning salons in my town.

This book is my life work of how I developed 9 simple steps that took me from a **war zone** salon owner to a **lifestyle** salon owner living in a beach house next to the Pacific Ocean. You too have the opportunity I had by reading this book and implementing these 9 simple steps in your salon.

New times are ahead and you can either embrace the change or you will be left behind,

Are you ready to learn the new way to grow your salon?

Let's do this…

Chapter 1 ATTRACT

Imagine standing outside your salon, and you can see through the window and it's pumping in there, every staff member is busy looking after the clients, the phone is ringing off the hook, you walk through the door and there's an upbeat vibe going on in the salon. You can hear the banter between the staff and the clients, the staff are happy and smiling, the clients are happy and you just sit there and take it all in. You have finally created the salon of your dreams. You take a look at the appointment book and it's full, actually it's overflowing. You've got high paying clients willing to pay a lot of money to visit your salon and everyone knows you are the best salon in town. Your staff get paid enough to buy a house and reach their dreams. Your bank account is healthy, all of the bills are up to date and you have your holidays booked already this year. You get to look after your special clients on the two days you work in the salon, and you're not working 70 hours a week anymore.

Your new role is to drive the salon business forward, you've made the step from apprentice to hairdresser or beautician, and then the next step to manager and then the big step to salon owner and now it's time for the final progression, to be the driver of the business, to make it successful.

Most of you probably think that's a far cry from reality at the moment. I used to think that too. Many years ago when I was an apprentice it was very easy for salon owners to make money and get their salons successful, there was a lot less competition then than there is today, which makes it a lot harder than most people think.

The simple fact is, that no salon will survive without clients.

Without fresh new clients coming into your salon on a regular basis your salon will always struggle. You need to realise that the game has changed. The world outside the salon has evolved. Most people don't realise this but it's not the same as it was. With the invention of social media, iPhones and Google we all thought that it would make it easier to attract clients to our salon without the expense of a Yellow Pages ad, leaflets or newspaper adverts, which were always very expensive.

How wrong we were!

What most salon owners don't realise is that because it's so easy to post on social media, it's actually easy for everybody, and now everyone's posting their work on social media, everyone's putting their before and after pictures out there, everyone's trying to advertise on social media which means that your pictures and your posts aren't getting seen anymore by the people that need to see them.

It has become a very, very crowded place. Seth Godin, who's a great motivator and coach quotes that if you're driving down the road and you see a purple cow it will stand out and you may even stare at it, but if the field were full of purple cows you would think that it wasn't so special and you would just switch off, not even notice it any more. And that's the same for your clients, they are switching off from your work because they've seen it so many times before on other peoples pages.

That's why it's so hard and you may be struggling to attract clients to your salon because people aren't seeing any of your posts any more, you might as well have just chucked them on the floor or put them straight in the bin.

It's one finger flick away from never being seen again, they last about 30 seconds, and all that effort you've put into creating that post becomes history.

What would be better is if you were able to send that post or that message out and it goes directly to that person that you're targeting and they see your post and they go, "Wow, where have you been all my life? I cannot believe I've been looking and searching for you all this time". The message catches their eye and they know you're the salon for them.

Imagine putting the right posts out there, or doing a leaflet drop, and the phone rings almost instantly and people want to come to your salon, and pay you whatever you charge with no complaints.

It means you can do less specials, it means less discounting but it all comes down to getting people to know you exist, to know you are the 'best kept secret' in town!

And that's something to be proud of!

If you are anything like me and you don't have a simple plan of action, you end up procrastinating and getting nothing done. I need clear and simple steps to follow which keeps me on the right track.

You need a plan of your salon dream, where and how your salon will be when it's finished, when you can say, "I'm done, this is the exact salon that I wanted to create".

Well, the easiest way I found is to track simple numbers (as salon owners we generally hate maths, I know I did) that you can relate to every day, like the clients average bill, and number of client visits per week. Really simple stuff and your staff can also track these numbers. If you know your exact numbers that will grow your salon business then it becomes very clear what actions you need to take today, and by when it needs to happen, you need to spend some time driving your salon business so you're not just putting fires out all day.

So you need to learn how to make ads and posts that get attention, so that the new clients who are looking for you can find you with ease. But if you're anything like me trying to figure out what to post, and when to post it, what pictures to use I end up sitting on a computer for hours and hours searching and nothing actually gets done, or worse I'm searching Photostock for a photo and 3 hours later, I get bored and put it in the too hard basket.

You see you've got to have some sort of rhythm, some sort of accountability that will make you realise that doing some marketing regularly is important to the salons growth. If people are looking for you now, you need to post regularly so that they know you're there, when they see your post for the first time most people will NOT do anything but when they are ready you will be the person they think of.

If you don't have a pattern then you'll just post when you're quiet, and when you're busy you'll stop. What we want is to have a plan of action so the marketing gets done whether you are quiet or busy.

Without fresh new clients in your salon your business will die, so let's learn how to make some noise, get seen and actually get clients.

Authority

Being a salon owner in todays world is scary, with a lot of you struggling to cover bills and paying your staff correctly, and then there's the added pressure of your cash flow being so tight, you're desperate to get clients in your salon fast. You even resort to heavily discounting your prices to make this happen. This is the start of your demise and takes you further and further into the **War Zone.**

I call it a **War Zone** because we have hundreds and thousands of salons trying to attract the same clients, with the same discounts, all having the same problems. They cannot find clients or staff to fill their salons and they are only one bad month away from closing their doors. They have zero back up cash to help them, with most of them putting in their own savings to keep their salon afloat.

Todays salon owners are a far cry from many years ago. We have the small boutique salons in the back garden of homes, we have 'rent a chair' owners, smaller salons in the high street employing just one or two staff members and being happy to stay small, we also have salon suites (smaller salons that bunch together under one building), mobile hairdressers, we have big chains of salons in the shopping centres, and also we have staff that are doing hair in their homes on their day off for extra cash. It's a different world, and you need to be aware that this change is NOT a fad, it's here to last. So you need to be more savvy than ever.

With so many salons and so much choice it's getter harder and harder to really book your salon out. It's actually hard to attract any new clients to your salon at all.

But this is not going to change, in fact I predict it will get worse before it gets better.

Workers want more freedom, they want to work less hours and get paid more, just like you do.

If you don't adapt and help them reach their goals, your employees will leave you and set up their own salon.

Just like you did!

That's what is happening right now. The world has changed outside your salon and you need to change with it. Or there will be more salons in your town chasing more of your clients.

You need to break away from the other salons in your area, and make your salon stand out, let me explain:

Clients are looking for new salons all the time.

How many new clients do you see in a week?

They have come from somewhere?

But the problem we are seeing is that the clients don't know why they should choose you. Many years ago we had good salons and bad salons, but today most salons are pretty good, it doesn't matter if you're a home salon, a high street salon, or a chain salon, the skills are the same and so is the experience that they offer.

In fact stop reading just now and answer the following questions:

If I was new to your town and I was looking for a new hairdresser or beautician, would I choose you?

Would you be different from the others?

Would I find you if I looked for a blonde hair expert or a facial expert?

Would I know that you were the best, or even a salon that could fix my biggest problem?

In the clients eyes when they're looking for a new salon they don't see many salons that stand out from anyone else. They all look the same, you all say you are good, you all say you're friendly, you all say you're colour experts, you all say that you are nail experts.

So the only way a client can choose which salon they will go to is on price.

And the desperate salon owner in the **War Zone** is happy to oblige, if it means the client chooses their salon.

So the **War Zone** is a vicious circle where salon owners are trying to get clients in using discounts because they know that's what they're looking for, and clients can only judge salon owners and salons on price so they're looking for discounts too.

That's why most salons never leave the **War Zone**. It's a never ending battle of salon owners trying bigger discounts and 'buy now pay later' schemes to attract clients to their salons, it's the only thing that they know works.

I want to share with you a new way, a simple way to attract clients to your salon that don't care about price. In fact they don't care how long the wait is, how much you charge or even which staff member is doing it.

You need to be 'the expert'.
You need to set your salon apart from every salon in town.
So price is not the driving force.
Every new client that comes to your salon has a problem that the previous salon didn't fix.
You need to learn more about that problem than anyone else and

be the expert in that subject.

Every time you do a consultation in your salon, you know that that client has come to you from another salon with something that's wrong.

It could be:

Their colour is too yellow
The other salon makes them wait
It takes too long
The greys are not covered
The hair cut doesn't last
The nails fall off

They all have a problem, listen at your next consultation and see if you can spot what is annoying them enough to leave their previous salon.

That is their biggest problem and your job is to solve that problem, whatever it may be, solve it and you have a client for life.

So what would happen if you could possibly write to these people before they go looking for a new salon and say, "Hey I know you have this problem and I am the expert in that problem, would you like me to fix this for you?".

Do you think that client will come to you on price or come to your salon because you can fix their problem?

I know for a fact that price is not an issue for that particular client, they just want their problem fixed.

So you have two options right now the old way or the new way

Now let's imagine that the clients are mice and we want to catch as many mice as possible, there are two ways in which we can do this. We can either hunt and chase them like the cat, or we can be a big block of tasty cheese, which the mice will come looking for, I want you to be the cheese and not the cat.

But many salon owners want to stay in the old way, it's easier, it's familiar, they don't have to learn new ways and they are happy to discount to get the clients in the door. We call them the 'CATS', they like hunting for clients all day, they like doing all the work, they like being busy chasing clients and don't want to work smarter, they're the one doing all the chasing with discounts all the time, they're the ones who are out there doing special offers, Groupon and so forth.

But many salon owners I coach are not like the 'CATS', they like to grow their salons smarter, they want the salon to be busy not just them. They want to concentrate on giving love to their clients and staff and don't really want to be hunting all day. They don't like the stress of the **War Zone** and want more purpose in life than just being busy. We call them the 'CHEESE'.

So the savvy salon owner of today wants to build a salon destination where it's all about the salon culture and team work, they tell their clients that they are there to fix their problems and give them love.

They show clients that they are the experts and prove that they can fix their problems, then the mice search for the cheese, the clients search for your salon.

So you have a choice today to choose to continually be the cat, hunting clients all day long, or you can be the tasty cheese and the clients will come to you, because they know that you're the best.

Many years ago when good quality salons had less good quality salons to compete with, all you had to do was have good trained staff, and it was really easy to fill the salon. You had the good salons who were often referred to as 'the big boys', they were upmarket, expensive and trained frequently and by the best. Then there were the smaller salons who were less expensive, you might even say they were cheap, their training was not very frequent, if at all in some cases, training costs money and these salons didn't have the spare cash that 'the big boys' had! The clients knew which salon they wanted to go to and it was easy for them to decide and people recommended you, they talked about you all day long and recommended their friends to go to 'their' salon.

But that was then and this is now!

Now everybody wants to own a salon, and it's much easier to open in your home, or in a suite, or even rent a chair, and the problem is all these salons are chasing the same clients, your clients.

Resulting in the **War Zone**, everyone trying to under cut each other to get ahead.

You can see the **War Zone**, it's full of salons all after the same clients, well that zone many years ago was almost empty with salons and there was plenty of clients to go around.

Tip: The ratio of people to salon is 2000:1

The average salon needs 2000 people living in their town per salon to make a good living.

Check the last census to see how many people live in your town, then add up all the salons in your area. Divide the salons by people and see how close you are to 2000, my salon only had an average of 456 people, I knew I had a fight on my hands just to survive. So I knew I could not afford to be average I had to be different from the rest. I didn't want to fight over clients on price.

So I became the expert (the cheese) and clients sought me out.

Imagine that the salons are fishing boats all going out to sea to catch fish for their supper, the **War Zone** is crowded with boats all after the same fish, but as you and I know there are only so many fish in that zone. So you're out there continually fishing over and over again to get just a little bit of reward.

But check out the deep blue ocean zone, that's not full of boats (salons). If you could paddle a little further out the sea is deep and the fish (clients) are plentiful, it's like learning new ways to actually get your salon busy again, like being an expert, to be the authority in town. Everybody wants to go to the best, no matter what you do, people will pay more for an expert to fix their problems. The best charge more for a start, and the best fixes their problem which is what we all want.

It's simple to get to the deep blue sea but it's not easy. Not many people are willing to put in the effort to get there, but that also means that it will never be over crowded, it will always have lots of fish (clients). Just start to set yourself up as an expert and your salon will be different from everyone else's in town. You're not there doing specials like everyone else, you're different and clients can see that, you're out there saying to the fish, "Come to me I can solve your problem, this is what I do and who I help", and they're just swimming into your nets, happy days!

Simple, but not easy, otherwise everyone would be doing it.

Most people prefer the easiest route.

Be that expert. You get better quality clients that seek out experts, they're willing to pay a lot more, and if they know that you're an expert in what they want they will stay around for longer because they're not going to be pulled away by the latest special.

The salon owner who attracts clients the old way by being cheap are always in danger of losing their clients to other salon owners who are cheap.

If you're not the cheapest salon in town then they may well leave you at any time and go to somebody else, if they came to you because you put a special on or a package together to get them through the door then you should know that another salon putting the same package or discount out there will attract that client to them, then they're going to leave you and go to that salon. They are not loyal one bit.

Also how can you expect your staff to hit their targets, I'm sure you will moan at them because they can't hit their targets every week. No client loyalty means their rebooks will be low and you'll nag them because their rebooks are so poor, but these people aren't rebooking because they're waiting for the next salon to give them a special, or for you to give them another special .

Your staff will be unhappy and you will put pressure on them that may result in them moving to another salon or giving up their profession for good.

They will never be able to hit 3 times their wage and it's imperative that your staff hit 3 times their wage for your profit to be good, that's one of the key numbers that you need to survive in todays salon world. Your wage bill needs to be as low as possible, 30% wage bill is the golden amount. That way there will be enough in the pot at the end of the year to pay yourself a good wage.

But also if you are the expert your salon becomes the destination for staff that are looking for a good job, who would not want to work at a place that's always busy, that are experts in what they do, not just average like the other salons, they will know that the people who work there get paid good wages because they're busy and everyones hitting their targets.

Your staff will stay around longer, why would they leave? The staff will find it easy to hit their targets, their rebooks will go up, their retail sales will go up, they will be doing all the nice clients, good paying clients that sought your salon out. Because your new clients have come to you because you are the expert, the best in town and you have solved their problem, and they know you love to make them happy, this will result in clients staying loyal longer, staff will stay longer and the clients will not be pulled away with special offers from the salon down the road.

When I opened my first salon I had to enter competitions and win awards, get myself in newspapers or famous magazines to attract these type of clients but nowadays you are so lucky, it's all about telling your story and backing it up.

Imagine if when you post your message on Facebook and the correct person gets to see it and wants what you offer. They know that you are the one.

Using whatever is most comfortable for you, video, Facebook, Instagram,Twitter, wherever you believe that your clients are gathered, it makes it really easy for you to talk to them directly and say to them, "Hey I know you suffer from this problem and we are experts at this and here's the proof, come and check us out, we are the salon that you have been looking and longing for"!

This is not the time to be the best kept secret in town, you need to get your message out there to the clients you are meant to serve, they're looking for you right now.

So many clients today are looking for a salon to call home, they're not price driven, they actually want to pay a good price for a good job.

The problem most salon owners have is that they don't know how to do this so they just do what they always have done and that means specials, attracting clients on price.

Learning to be the authority in your town, be the best in your clients world.

If you get this right and put a little more effort into paddling out to the deep blue sea, you will attract good, loyal clients.

Imagine a group of girlfriends out having coffee and one of them says, "I have this problem", and the girlfriends say, "Go and see Richards salon, he's an expert in that". They know they've read it somewhere and it almost becomes the truth.

Start this today as you do your next consultation in your salon, write it down.

Build a list of all the clients problems and use them for content for your next post, blog, video or marketing campaign.

Take a look at this case study, of a salon owner that I work with, this salon owner was just like everybody else who used to put specials out and decided that he was going to be an authority in his field in his town.

Let's take a look at him

CASE STUDY

I really needed something to wake me up, i had lost both my parents very recently , especially my mum Nancy who had also been my mentor in her earlier days with over 10 very successful salons, while watching one of Richard McCabes webinars he said something which really resinated with me , sometimes you have to draw a line !!!!!

What I started to realise very quickly was how much I wasn't doing , things I had let slip , I had lost direction and was going round in circles ,its amazing that my business was still profitable . Richards program is really helping me put systems in place that I believe will grow my business but more importantly makes me realise why have been in this industry for 40 years, its my passion and thanks to Richard I'm getting it sorted . I would strongly recommend this course, it will help you in so many ways, I am still amazed how far you can refine systems and do advertising that works I have only been doing the course for a few weeks and my team and I are so excited with the results !!!

Thanks so much Richard
Mark Gower, Gosh Hair Studio, Queensland, Australia

Money Map

With so many salons sitting in the **War Zone**, fighting for new clients, fighting for staff and fighting to increase their takings, I don't just want to help you get out of the **War Zone**, I want you to fly out of it. It's so hard to focus on what actually needs to get done to grow your salon with the hundreds of things that can happen every day to take away your focus and time, your salon needs enough growth to leave the **War Zone** behind and start enjoying life again in the **Lifestyle Zone**. You need to get yourself out of the **War Zone** as quickly as possible and that's done by adding a massive percentage growth in 12 months.

When I say massive, I mean a massive 30%!

Increasing your salons turnover by 30% will have a massive impact on your salon and your life. It's enough for most salons to leave the **War Zone** and start breathing again.

A 30% growth is really simple to achieve and is very, very achievable in a 12 month time frame if you have clarity and focus on what actions you need to take.

You might think if I build my salon to be great, make it look fantastic and beautiful, the clients will come. They will not, this is such an old fashioned way of thinking.

Some salon owners still believe that giving referral cards out to clients and saying, "Pass these on to your friends", will make clients come in the door, this is so old fashioned. Clients don't want to send their friends in to you, just in case you mess up, it's too risky for them. Anyway I prefer to be in control rather than hope that a client I handed a bunch of cards to will one day pass them on. I want to be in control of how clients find me, that way I can control the outcome.

You need a plan, if you have no plan that means you will probably end up with no growth, and if you have no growth then your salon is slowly dying.

Your role as a salon owner is to work out what are the simple numbers that will have the biggest impact on your salons takings, and share this information with your team. Someone once said to me, "If you think it, ink it", get it written down, it becomes more believable and true, and gives you a step by step guide of how to actually achieve this.

It's a lot easier than you think.

By now you should know there are only 3 ways to grow your salon:

Attract more clients to your salon
Convert these clients to visit more often
Deliver a remarkable service so the clients will spend more

But if there are only 3 ways then why are so many salons still stuck in the **War Zone.**

I believe it's down to foggy thinking, too much to do, and that means nothing gets done.

Clarity is king.

Most salons that try to increase their takings will do so by just concentrating on only one of the 3 ways to grow any business. **Attracting** 30% new clients to the salon is almost impossible, if an average salon looks after 100 clients per week that means finding 30 more clients per week, that's over 1500 per year. That's pretty hard to do and besides, you will need more staff to achieve this.

To try and **Convert** your clients to visit you sooner by 30% is a tall feat also. That's like getting your existing clients who visit every 6 weeks to rebook in every 4 weeks, do you think you could do that?

And getting your team to **Deliver** a remarkable service to increase the retail and service bill from $100 to $130 with every client is pretty impossible in such a small time frame without losing clients, because they feel you are pushing them to buy.

That's why people never achieve this and get confused, misled and give up. To take your salon to a 30% increase in one area of your business is pretty hard to do by anyone's standard. So if that was you don't feel too hard done by, because as you now see it's near impossible to achieve.

But it's so much more achievable if you do it in smaller bites and you work on all 3 areas at once, this will supersonic your growth, faster than you could ever imagine.

Sounds complicated?

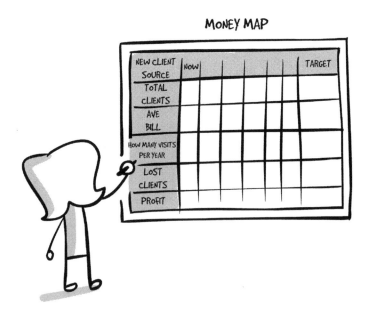

Not at all! With the money map everything becomes crystal clear so you can focus on what needs to happen.

Next we're going to take you through what we call the money map model. Just familiarise yourself with the money map picture below and see that there are 5 sections going down and 7 boxes across the top.

So let's be brave, you bought this book to learn a new way to grow your salon and by the end of this book you will have the same tools I had to take my salon into the lifestyle salon and hundreds of salons around the world have had and now they are all enjoying the lifestyle that they dreamed of.

Let's set a goal, a big huge goal, to get you a 30% or higher increase in takings within 12 months time.

The secret is to break down each section to know exactly how many clients you need, what they need to spend, and how often they must visit you. The money map model will show you exactly what you have to do to achieve this goal in such an easy step by step way, you'll think it's too easy to be true.

By just adding 30% to your takings and saying, "This is my goal for the year", will not cut it. You and I both know that a goal without a plan is just a dream. And we are not dreaming here, it's real and you are going to achieve this and change the way you operate your salon forever.

Think about running a marathon. If you don't know if you can possibly do that marathon or how long it's going to take you or where the water stops are or when you can have breathers or when you can walk and when you can run and how far you've travelled.

If you just literally started and ran and said, "I'm going to run a marathon", there's a good chance that you're going to give up, your mind will give up before your body does. They say it's all in the head, well I believe that to be true for big goals too. If I know they are broken down into small enough steps so that I can say, "Yes" that's simple, I can do that", and I will probably smash it too. If you have a step by step plan that you know you can achieve and have the exact number that you need to grow your business it means that you've got something to aim for every single week until you hit it, you'll be amazed at how easy it actually is.

Let's break that 30% down into smaller bites and let's use what we already know to be true.

We know there are only 3 ways to grow your business:

Attract more clients to your salon
Convert these clients to visit more often
Deliver a remarkable service so the clients spend more

What if we worked on each one and increased the amount by 10% for each of them?

That's doable right?

Let's **Attract** 10% more clients
Convert your clients to come in 10% sooner
And **Deliver** a great service that your average bill goes up 10% too

That now gives us a simple goal to start us off with and it seems simple to get to.

New clients

Take a look at this example in the money map below of a salon with a turnover of $400,000, if they do an average of 100 clients per week then we'll aim for them to do 110 clients per week, just 10 more clients per week, that's not a lot.

MONEY MAP

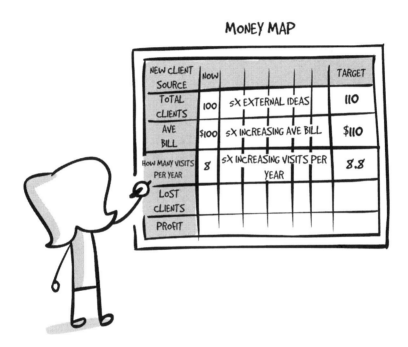

NEW CLIENT SOURCE	NOW						TARGET
TOTAL CLIENTS	100	5x EXTERNAL IDEAS					110
AVE BILL	$100	5x INCREASING AVE BILL					$110
HOW MANY VISITS PER YEAR	8	5x INCREASING VISITS PER YEAR					8.8
LOST CLIENTS							
PROFIT							

If you've got an average of 3 staff that's really 3 clients per staff member, very, very doable.

Get them spending more

If the clients who visited the salon had an average bill of $100 we'll set the goal for the average bill to $110, a $10 increase, that's only half a retail product, that's a third of a treatment, you could even put your prices up by 5% and you've only got 5% to find now, very, very achievable.

Get them in sooner

If this salons client visits are around 8 times per year and you aim to get them to visit 8.8 times a year, it's so doable, and that'll give you another 10% increase in your business.

But those small 10% increases as you will see are massive, to a salon that's turning over $400,000 that's an extra $120,000 increase in 12 months, that takes them to $520,000, really achievable and such a massive impact to your top line and to your profit.

You see we know now what numbers are important and the old saying, "How do you eat an elephant?", "One bit at a time". It's the simple steps that you do on a continual, regular basis that makes the difference.

Trying to go after a 30% increase in new clients, I don't think you'd achieve it, in fact I know it's virtually impossible unless you're throwing specials all over the place and then the clients wont stay around for long.

By not planning your salons growth you will just plod along until something gives, and that something is usually you. If you don't increase your takings per year, your salon bills will increase, your staff will want pay rises, your stock will go up and no increase in takings will mean there's no money for a refit, your salon will start to look shabby, and I'm not talking 'shabby chic', I'm talking 'shabby tatty'. Clients will then think that you're a bit shabby, your staff don't want to work at a shabby place. Your staff will eventually ask for more money over time and you wont be able to afford to give it to them, they will resent you and the salon. It's demoralising for you, your passion which got you this far will start fading and you are the only person driving this business and if you start fading then the salon starts fading.

As we all know, your wage bill will go up and general bills will go up and if your takings remain the same, the only person that's losing out is you, because the staff will still get paid, the stock will still get paid, the rent will still get paid, it means that you will be last and pay yourself less.

Take a look at the picture of the money map above, I use this with my private coaching clients it will help you break down those big goals into small manageable bites that makes it so simple to achieve.

Let's check out this salons numbers first using the example that I just gave you, then you can work out your salons goal.

You will notice that in the 'NOW' section this particular salon does 100 TOTAL CLIENTS per week

They have an AVERAGE BILL of $100

AND VISIT the salon 8 times a year

Under the target section you will see that this salon has added their 10% increase to each individual section, hoping to achieve their goal in 12 months.

The target for TOTAL CLIENTS is now 110

The target for AVERAGE BILL is now $110

The VISITS per year is now 8.8 times

Now let's work out your salon targets, download the money map template here:

https://isaloncoaching.lpages.co/money-map/

What are the numbers going on in your salon right now, what's your starting point?

Dive into your computer system and find out how many clients your salon does on average every week? It's best if you take an average over a full year and divide it by 52 weeks.

For your average bill, work out your 12 months takings and divide this amount with your 12 months clients visits, this will give you your salons total AVERAGE BILL

$$\text{Average client bill} = \frac{\text{takings}}{\text{client visits}}$$

$$\text{Average client visits} = \frac{\text{total clients}}{\text{individual clients}}$$

For your average CLIENT VISITS work out how many total client visits you had (as some clients visit you more than once per year) and divide that amount by how many individual clients visited during that period.

Then let's look at making you a 30% increase.

Add 10% to the numbers you have, that should give you your goal. Go ahead and write the target on the money map.

I want to tell you about the day that I implemented this in my salon.

I had a crystal clear plan from day one, which made it so easy for me to track the right numbers that actually grow your business and I could share it with my team. We tracked it daily, weekly, monthly and quarterly. It got me excited as I started hitting these numbers really quickly. It jumped my business up by 33% in 12 months and that changed my life, 33% increase was all it took to feel safe and secure, to escape the feast and famine of irregular monthly takings.

I managed to replicate that increase again and again, year on year. Really simple stuff but life changing results. This crystal clear clarity, these simple 10% targets are going to change your salon too, the lives of your staff and your life, forever. This is going to catapult you into a lifestyle salon, faster than you ever thought possible.

Looking at the money map picture again you will see you have your starting point (where you are now) and your target numbers.

In between you will see 5 boxes across in a row of each category.

You see just writing down your targeted amount isn't enough to make it happen, you can use all the manifestation you want, it isn't going to happen on its own.

You need action points to make the numbers grow.

What's really interesting and really simple to understand is the top row when we're talking about attracting new clients, we just need 5 simple projects aiming externally from the salon.

So that means you're going to be doing maybe Facebook posts or ads,

Instagram, leaflets, or even 5 external projects you are going to work on throughout the year to attract new clients in the door.

Can you think of ways to attract clients in your salon. Add them to your money map.

The next row is for INCREASING AVERAGE BILL getting clients to spend more, getting your average bill up. You're going to work on just 5 simple strategies, 5 simple projects, maybe you'll do some internal training with the staff on consultations, maybe you'll do some retail training, maybe you'll do some internal offers or cross promotions for clients.

Now add your ideas to the 5 boxes in increasing AVERAGE BILL

The last section you need to work on is increase the amount of VISITS in a year, five simple internal projects to get the clients to return sooner. You are going to use your salons database that's actually in your computer system and do 5 simple projects to get them returning sooner.

You could offer them, discounts for quieter days, bundle a package to overdue clients, you might also do an email campaign on major events of the year and make a package around it, Halloween, Christmas, Mothers Day, Valentines Day and you can plan this way ahead of time.

Three simple ways to grow your salon, 5 simple projects to reach that 10% increase goal.

It's much easier than you think when you have a clear and concise plan that starts off at your bigger picture dream and adding a 30% increase to your business will make it happen faster.

Then breaking down that 30% total takings increase and bringing it down to a simple and easy lower level, to action points.

When you know exactly, per week how many clients you need to get in, what they need to spend and how often they need to return, it makes it crystal clear what you have to do to make that happen.

Remember the only 3 ways to grow your business:

Attract more clients to your salon
Convert these clients to visit more often
Deliver a remarkable service so the clients spend more

At Lifestyle Salon Coaching you will notice that we only teach you what it takes to grow your business and nothing else.

Keep It Simple...

CASE STUDY

So even though Richard is located on the other side of the world from me, he has been absolutely great. By this i mean with his history and past of his ups and downs he does keep it real and to the point. If things don't go to plan or things don't change there is only one person to blame and that is, " Yourself"

If ever i have questions or need help he's there even though he's 11 hours ahead. The great quality with Richard is- He's direct and blunt (NO BULLSHIT).

Also Richard creating this close family community of salon and spa owners, this is a great forum where if you need help or opinions 24/7 form other owners we are there for each other.

Onay Mehmed, Lounge Salon Hair & Beauty, London, UK

Marketing Mastery

On January 1st millions of people around the world declare to their friends and family that this year is going to be different. They say goodbye to their bad habits and behaviours, and they make a promise that this New Year will be different to the rest!

They make their resolution to lose weight, be healthier, stop smoking, to go for a run every day, join the gym, drop a dress size, be more successful and promise to have a better year than the last. Whatever it may be, they declare to their friends and family that this is their year it's going to happen this time.

But did you know that only 8% of people actually keep their New Years resolutions. That's an astonishing 92% of people who fail every year, who never follow through to actually do what they promise they said they would do.

It's not for lack of trying, they really want to achieve this, but it's hard. That's why we attract so many salon owners joining us at the Lifestyle Salon Coach, because they need that accountability to keep them motivated when things get tough. I'm sure you are the same!

So when it comes to your marketing you need to make it part of your daily routine, like brushing your teeth. Finding a rhythm that works for you is the key, because if you are like me and maybe other salon owners, it soon becomes a nuisance or a pain to remember when to post.

Most of us, myself included have these great ideas and we say, "I'm going to do something about this situation", and before you know it you've stopped. You become busy and it's all forgotten. All it takes is a staff member calling in sick, or a client that may have turned up late, you may have just gotten busy, the salon would get busy, your life would get busy and all the marketing would just seem unimportant at that time. We all get busy and then tend to fall back into our old, bad ways.

On average it's stated that it takes 21 days to break a bad habit and 66 days to start a new one.

So we need a plan to make this a priority, because if you can build momentum in your salon, your salon will grow FAST and STRONG, without too much effort.

In fact we all have the same 24 hours in the day. Richard Branson, Steve Jobs, Mark Zuckerberg, you get the drift.

So if they can manage to grow successful businesses so can you.

To grow your business is simpler than you think, you know it's down to only 3 ways:

    Attract new clients
    Convert them to visit more often
    Deliver a remarkable service to increase their average spend

You just need a system that helps you to target these 3 ways without forgetting anything, getting overwhelmed, or just becoming too busy to do it.

Most salon owners only start looking for new clients when they are quiet and see gaps appear in their appointment book, most would only market their business when it's needed. But, by then it's too late!

It's almost impossible to try and attract clients to your salon instantly, without giving away a massive discount. Wouldn't it be great if clients would ring the salon when we needed them?

There is a time and place to offer discounts, which I'll cover later on. But for now we want your salon busy with high paying clients and they are not sitting there waiting for you to call them.

Trying to attract clients only when you're quiet is the old way but that's still what most salon owners do, I don't want you to be one of them. They see a gap in their appointment book and they panic. They throw out a special offer to get clients in quickly, sometimes it works, sometimes it doesn't. If it doesn't they put out another special, or give up saying, "Facebook doesn't work for me".

Then two or three weeks down the line gaps appear in the appointment book again or a bill is due, and they panic and they start marketing again.

We call that helicopter marketing, it means you're just marketing here and there whenever you need it, up and down, up and down.

If you want to get your salon really busy in today's modern world you need 'momentum'.

Really good paying clients will not leave their current salon until they have found another salon to go to, so right now your prospective client is checking you out (we'll cover this in more detail in the next chapter). But you need to market your salon every single day, even when you don't need clients.

If you have ever made a giant snowman you know exactly what I'm talking about. Imagine pushing a giant snowball up a hill it's hard work, in fact it is muscle draining hard, but it's not impossible.

When I was a child my friends and I would run outside in the garden and we would get to build this giant snowball, it would start off really small and we would roll it and roll it and roll it until it was bigger than my friends and I.

Then my friends would help and join in and we would roll it, roll it, and roll it some more and it would grow to be as big as a car. We would push it all over the place thinking it was hilarious, eventually we would stop to take a breather and that was it, we couldn't move it, it just wouldn't budge. But while we were pushing it and kept it moving, it seemed easy to move around, but the minute we stopped it took so much effort to get that snowball moving again, we would eventually give up.

That's the same as your salon marketing, when you start marketing your salon, nothing happens, then all of a sudden the phone rings and a couple of clients book in, and a few more and as you start attracting more clients to your salon the flow keeps on going.

It seems easy, right?

But that's when most salon owners do the worst thing ever, they stop, they think their job is done. They stop the advert that was working so well and this stops the momentum. They just didn't realise, or they forgot that the advert didn't just work there and then it took time to get that first client to respond to the ad.

When you start marketing or you're positive about marketing and clients start coming, I don't think it's manifestation I think it's the fact that you're actually doing something. Being proactive as opposed to reactive.

First you need to discover your marketing mode, then you need to discover your marketing rhythm.

Your marketing mode

This is where you choose what form of marketing you want to send out. This is important because each form offers a different result, so it's dependant on what result you want to achieve.

Let's explore the 3 main marketing modes:

PASSIVE

Passive marketing is where you put your work out there with no call to action. You just put your work out to say, "We're experts in this particular service, come and check us out, here is some proof about what we do, we know you have a problem, this is how we fix it." It's a bit like whispering in someones ear, "Hey come and check us out, we are good at this".

You would use this if your salon is full, to keep front of mind with prospective clients, so when they are ready to make the move from their old salon you are always front of mind. This is also good to use on your website. This mode generally does not cost you anything, it's not an advert, and it works passively in the background.

ACTIVE

Active is where you are actively looking for fresh new clients for your salon, making a bit more noise so people take notice of you. It's about talking a little more loudly to them as opposed to whispering in their ear.

It might have a call to action, it might have a show and tell, it might have some before and afters and fixing of their problems. Your call to action might be, 'call this number now' or 'we have vacancies on Monday'. It's a little bit more active, you're actively looking for clients in this mode. I would use this active mode to attract clients to my salon for my quietest staff members. I would also use this active mode if I were going to do a Valentines day, Halloween, or Christmas promotion. I'm actively looking for some new clients, I have a few holes in my appointment book, I'm trying to pump up a quiet month.

HYPERACTIVE

Hyperactive should be used with caution. If you're desperate, your cash flow is low, your bills need paying and you need clients now, then you need to give them the biggest reason to call your salon 'NOW' (a bribe).

What would get you calling a shop and buying today? 25% off, 50% off, 75% off?

If passive is whispering, and active is talking, hyperactive is screaming at people. It's saying, "Come in and get your hair done NOW". This is what I call 'get them in now, at all costs'. If your staff have no clients then go into hyperactive mode, if you have days that are dead like when there's only 1 client booked in, then go into a hyperactive mode and get them calling the salon today. Give them whatever it takes to make this happen, even 100% off, FREE (I gave this advice to one of my coaching clients to book out a particular day, it took her two weeks to be fully booked on that day with full paying clients).

I would say hyperactive is totally worth going into if you have a really high rebooking rate, because you know once you get them into the salon you're going to win them over.

Now depending on how desperate you are or how busy your salon is, if your staff are busy, you move in and out of passive, active and hyperactive depending on your needs. You could run passive ads all week and hyperactives just for one staff member.

You can move between different modes whenever you need, you get to turn that client attraction tap on and off whenever you want.

When you employ a new stylist it's a good idea to go into hyperactive mode to get them busy FAST, as they get busier with more clients, you can back off a little and move into active mode and once they're fully booked move into passive mode, that's how I grew my salon team to be fully booked.

Your Marketing Rhythm

Everything you do is either attracting or repelling your prospective clients.

If you are anything like I was, I would sit in front of a computer and I didn't know what to write, or I would just get around to it when I was quiet and then I would stop when I got busy.

I would post on a Friday sometimes and then I would forget until next Monday or get called away from the computer and forget what I was doing, or I'd leave it a couple of weeks, until I had time. I didn't really know what I was doing, I'd just throw any stuff out there and hope it worked, hope that people would call the salon, I never had a plan.

I would only look for new clients if it was quiet and I would usually stick to what I did before, even though it didn't work the first time. I guess most of you are the same!

If you're anything like me, I'm easily distracted when I don't really commit myself to it and I move on quickly if I get bored, or I'll pass it on to somebody else, give it to any staff member to do. It just seems too hard sometimes and I just give up.

When I ask my salon owner clients about their marketing now, they say they have good intentions but they are always putting fires out all day long. It reminds me of what I did. Nothing practical! Nothing changed!

You may have great intentions, plan to book an hour out in your diary to actually do some marketing and all it takes is a staff member turning up late, or a client doesn't turn up at all and puts you in a bad mood and before you know it you're rushing around like an idiot and you're just putting fires out all day long, this pattern is typical of most salon owners and before you know it, 5 years have gone by and you've got no or little salon growth, and if you're not growing your salon is surely dying.

If you can organise yourself with a momentum accountability plan, it takes the pressure off you and you will know that you are working on your salons growth, even if you are doing multiple day to day tasks. Every single day that you get to tick it off your marketing planner, your salon is growing.

Book an hour in your diary today, to concentrate on your marketing every single week. And after a few weeks you should have broken your bad habits (bad habits of you sitting in the backroom gossiping, I know I did) and started a new good habit, a habit that actually grows your business. So go on, book it in your diary today, do it now, one hour per week and dedicate that to your marketing plan.

Remember everything you do is either attracting or repelling your prospective clients

Most of the time clients are not ready to make the move to your salon straight away, some will, some haven't fallen out with their present salon yet, and some that are maybe giving their current salon one more chance. And you want to be front of mind when they do decide it's time to move.

There are three types of clients that you are trying to attract, and remember they will come when they are ready. Your modes will play a big role here, but you need to talk to, and be in front of these people everyday if you can.

You need to make a commitment to actually post something, deliver an advert or send an email. Because you never know when these clients will be ready.

Only 3% of prospective clients are ready to buy now, that's not a lot. But they like the hyperactive mode.

67% of prospective clients are a little more cautious, these are the high paying clients and are checking you out, watching everything you do, they want to make sure that if they move to your salon, your salon is the right fit for them, so they need constant reassuring from you that your salon does what they want.

The rest, the 30% that are left are the die hard clients, you know the ones, they love you and will never leave you ever, these may never come to you. But even with your die hard clients some will eventually leave.

So I want you to aim for the biggest group, the 67% is what we are aiming for (Note: Not many salon owners bother to attract these clients, they prefer the 3% because it requires less work and it's easier)

That means you need to talk to them in passive or active mode every day if you can. You need a rhythm to keep you accountable.

Don't try and do too much, don't overload yourself with too much too soon, do what you can honestly do everyday without working yourself ragged, this is about you, holding yourself accountable to actually do it on a certain day and a certain time.

So where do your prospective clients hang out? Where can you show up to say, "Hi". And what time of the day do they look for you?

Once you know this then it's all about you planning your marketing accountability and just doing it.

Moving into your rhythm and your mode you get to speak to all these types.

Important: Read this story about a guy who goes into a bar, looking for a date.

This guy goes into a bar looking for a date and he's entered the bar walked straight up to two ladies, you notice him and he's quite good looking, and he whispers in their ears. Two minutes later he walks up to another girl and he whispers in her ear. Then he walks round the bar going to every girl and whispers in their ears. He's not looking very happy, and then he comes to you, it's your turn and he whispers in your ear and he says, "Hey, can I have your phone number", and you're thinking what a sleaze, there's no way I'm giving you my number.

He didn't even care about me enough to ask my name or even make an effort to get to know me. He just wanted action. He wanted you to say YES. But you're not desperate and you have no time for sleazy men. Even though one day he will get lucky with around 3% of the ladies he asks.

Most salons advertising and marketing are very similar to that sleazy guy in a bar. They aim for the 3% and don't have the time to build up a relationship. They want action now!

Imagine the same story but the guy is looking for a lasting relationship, the 67%. The same guy comes into the bar, he sits down and he overhears your conversation with your friend and you're talking about your dog. The guy says, "Hey I've got a dog, does your dog do this" and you go, "Yeah my dog does that". He finishes his drink and off he goes. Now next week he comes back in the bar and you're there again. He asks, "Hey how's your dog going", and you say, "Great thanks, hows yours", and he says, "Yeah he's good thanks". He asks, "Can I sit and chat", and you go, "Yeah, sure", and you sit and chat for an hour, and then he goes home.

A week after that and he comes in again and he says, "Hi", and you sit down and you carry on the conversation where you left off and then he says to you, "Can I have your number? I'd love to ask you out", and you go, "Sure". He seems like a nice guy.

You see that's what marketing should be like.

Good quality clients need to know and trust you and that takes some time to build up, that rapport, that communication, that story telling, that whatever it may be. It takes some time to do that and we call that momentum.

Great clients that spend well, don't move salons too often, they usually do their homework before they move salons and commit to them. These ARE the 67% and to think many salon owners don't have the patience or desire to put the work into them. This is an untapped market in the salon world.

I see so many salons doing specials and discounts aiming at the 3%, be different, stand out, put in the work and reap the rewards.

Don't be the sleazy person in the bar.
Remember use Hyperactive with caution!

That's like you just sending out specials saying to your clients, "I want you to come in now" and that's very similar to that guy, can I have your phone number now.

But the other way of course is building momentum, it's saying to your clients, "Hey this is us, we've set ourselves apart, this is what we do, would you like to come and try us out".

The best way to grow your salon is to move in and out of marketing modes to keep your posts and adverts interesting, and also to use these modes when you need them the most.

Gary Vaynerchuk wrote a book called 'Jab, Jab, Jab Right-Hook'. It was referring to a boxer, he would never just throw a right hook, as the opponent would know and get used to his moves, so he would throw a left, left, left, right hook to keep him on his guard. Well, that's the same as marketing, 'Passive, passive, passive active, passive, passive, passive, hyperactive. Keep them guessing.

How I filled my quiet days in the salon

I used hyperactive mode to fill my quiet days, I had two stylists who I just couldn't get filled on a Wednesday, everything I did just failed. It was the quietest day in the salon, so what I decided to do was move into hyperactive mode and I offered a half price colour with every full priced cut and blow dry. That got our Wednesdays fully booked, within a few months. We called it 'Wicked Wednesday'. Wednesday turned out to be one of our most popular days and was booked out months and months in advance. I was happy too as most of my clients moved from a Friday or a Saturday to fill the Wednesday and I filled the gaps on Fridays and Saturdays easily. Also the salon average bill wasn't too bad either at $130. When Wednesday was full, we then moved into passive mode which means we didn't advertise 'Wicked Wednesday' any more we went into a passive mode and just put a little blurb on the website.

By using this mode, it increased my average bill (for mid week), it freed up Friday and Saturday for fresh new clients, which increased my new clients percentage, and of course because they were all booked out my average visits per year went up too. I covered all three ways to grow any business with one campaign. Happy days!

How I used a hyperactive mode in my salon to fill 3 quiet months

I had 3 quiet months in the year. March, June and November, these months were not good for me they were quite frankly, rubbish. So I decided to do a hyperactive advertising campaign to fill these quiet months.

I brought a whole new service into the salon, a smoothing service.

We charged around $300 for this service. We decided to let all of our clients know internally with an email campaign. We didn't do an external advertising campaign with this one, it was an internal campaign so I was working on my Money Map bringing clients in sooner and also lifting the average bill.

I was working on 2 ways to grow my business in this hyperactive mode.

I offered the smoothing service with a discount of $100 off, that's a third off their bill, if you come in during those three quiet months, March, June and November.

So if they came in during these months they could have the service for $200, and of course I knew they would rebook to have it done again a few months later when it eventually faded out, because naturally why would they pay full price again.

I was happy giving away discount to turn a bad month into a good month, I had turned a month that used to take around $38000 into a month taking $44000, so I'm happy, my staff were happy because they were hitting their targets, I'm happy because I'm hitting my Money Map target, and my clients are happy because they are saving $100. It's a win, win for everybody.

By moving into hyperactive mode, giving money off I then made lots more money with a service that I didn't really offer at that time.

By the way, my average visits increase by 10% because of this campaigns success.

By keeping your marketing moving with a momentum, never stop even when you're fully booked, you will see your salon continually grow, all you need to do is go into passive mode, when you are fully booked.

If you can build a momentum and a rhythm with your marketing, you know exactly when you're marketing is going out and who you're talking to and what action you want them to take, then your salon will get booked out very, very soon, you'll book every single day out in your business, you wont have to worry about quiet days again, you wont have to worry about your staff not hitting their targets.

Knowing exactly what to post, when to post it, and what result you want to happen is what a true salon owner, leader is called to do.

Remember that snowball, DO NOT stop pushing that snowball up the hill otherwise it will be so hard to get it moving again.

CASE STUDY

WHAT MADE YOU JOIN US:

"I liked that you were no nonsense

You were clearly not willing to chase me, you didn't want my money if it wasn't right for you

You told me that I needed to McDonaldise my salon which I had been saying for a while now

I had no money and I was like"Paypal give me a day ahead before it clears, I'm doing this"

These were the main reasons"

WHAT WAS HOLDING YOU BACK FROM JOINING, WHAT WERE YOU A LITTLE SCARED OF:

"I'd signed a lease and I needed to make money

For me there wasn't much of a hesitation I just needed to find the right person, I was actively looking for someone to help me"

FROM THE WORK THAT YOU'VE DONE SO FAR, WHAT HAVE YOU LEARNT THAT YOU'VE LOVED:

"I absolutely love that momentum sheet, I print one out weekly and decorate it with washi tape and stick it in my journal

I really like the pink sheets, so far I've only used them for systemising in the salon (I'm not up to that module yet) and it made a huge difference for me, why we need to do something and how we do it"

Jackie Young, Jackie Renee Salon, United States

Chapter 2 CONVERT

CONVERT

The world outside your salon has changed, the clients have changed, the staff have changed and if you don't change with it you will be left behind. There are some savvy salon owners that are adapting and changing with the times, I have quite a few in my Lifestyle Salon System Program.

Don't be the salon owner that's left behind!

Many years ago it would be quite normal to overhear a group of ladies who were doing coffee together, talking about how much money they spent on a pair of shoes, or how much money they spent on a handbag, they didn't care how much it cost as long as it was the latest edition or on trend. They worked hard and spent hard. Then when the big recession hit, the conversations changed. It became trendy to now talk about how much money they had saved, even if they could afford to spend more, it was all about being a little more frugal with their money, they didn't want to offend anyone that was hit hard by the credit crunch.

We went through an era of 'whoever saved the most' was the savviest.

The tides are now turning back where people are happy to say, "I go to Richard's salon", knowing it's expensive and they're no longer embarrassed if it's costly. They are happy to show off their latest handbag again no matter the cost. But now there's a catch, they need to feel they've been given great value for money.

Master the experience with a great product and you will open your doors to the new money that's out there.

We all love Facebook likes, and Instagram hearts, it makes us feel warm and fuzzy, it makes us think that our marketing is working, that people like us.

You might think that your salon is doing well because you have 60,000 Instagram followers or 10,000 Facebook likes.

There's no point in having lots of likes on Facebook, lots of shares, lots of views, but no clients actually taking the next step. No one picking up the phone and calling your salon.

Try and pay your rent, or your tax bill with 'likes' or 'followers', it will not get you too far, 'likes' will not pay your bills, good old fashioned money will.

Therefore you need to convert as many of your 'likes' and 'followers' into real money as you can.

Using these 3 simple strategies to help you convert your likes on Facebook and direct them to your website, to try and win them over to eventually getting them into your salon as full paying clients with ease and with automation. We don't want you working any harder than you need to.

People today feel that they need to like and trust you. They are more wary than ever that salon owners are just trying to trick them to come into the salon, just doing a special and then to up sell them once they are in the salon.

So they will definitely go and check you out , they may like some of your pictures or your posts, but they need to feel a connection between them and you. So as they Google you or head to your website they will be looking for something, a connection of some kind. And this is where you get to convert that follower into a loyal client, an actual real person calling the salon and giving you money.

Customers today know that most salon owners are just trying to sell to them, that most salon owners are trying to get them in the door and that just doesn't work with good quality clients.

So there is an intangible pre client journey that you need to build in order to convert that prospect into a client.

You'll need to back up your story, show them a connection and make it easy for them to get in contact with you.

In fact we are being bombarded by around 5000 ads per day, no wonder people think we're lying or they're switching off. Everyone is trying to get their attention. So they want to be able to choose who they do life with. They want to choose who they spend their money with.

And the foundations of convert is about proving, backing up your story and saying, "I'm honest and true, and we really do believe in this, we can solve your problem".

Also you can use these same strategies in exactly the same way to attract new staff to your salon.

I hear so many salon owners at the moment that can't convert their job advertisement into people actually calling the salon or even emailing the salon, nothing, zilch not even one interview, and again the reason is, staff are also checking you out, so you need to make sure they get the right information needed.

I recently had a one to one coaching session with one of my clients and we built her an advert for her salon. We concentrated on her story and what the salon wanted to achieve, after no reply to her pervious adverts she was inundated with staff wanting to work for her. She took on 3 new additional staff within a week. Don't underestimate the power of letting people know what you stand for.

We need to make sure that we back up our story 110% with everything that we do.

So let's dive into convert and figure out how we can convert likes into money, convert clients into raving fans of your salon, and to convert your quietest days into your busiest days.

Win Them Over

Imagine your salons phone ringing off the hook with clients begging you to book them in. They don't even ask about how much you charge, they don't ask how long the wait is. They're just desperate to get their hair or beauty service needs done with your salon.

But the reality is different, it's just not like that in the real world.

The salon phone rings, you pick up the phone up and one of the first things the client says to you is, "How much is this going to cost", and you know instantly that price is a big issue for them.

What if you could put steps in place to turn off the clients that you don't want in your salon, you know the ones, the bargain hunters and discount chasers; and attract the right clients who are happy to pay good money for your services, how great would that be?

What if every time the phone rang in your salon it would be a client begging to do service with you, regardless of price?

Let me show you how that works in the real world.

Imagine a new client or a prospective client who hears about you or gets referred to you. First they'll drive past your salon, they'll see your advert, they'll see your posts, or they'll see anything to do with you, there will be a process that they will go through before they call the salon.

Many years ago clients would just call the salon or walk in on a whim and hopefully you looked after them and did a good job, but that was then and this is now. Clients are more savvy and WILL do their homework on you before they trust you to look after them.

It's far harder to get referrals or clients to believe in you, clients are far more savvy than they ever were before. They're going to check you out, they're going to Google you, Facebook you, Instagram you, even look at reviews about you and they're going to find out if your salon has what they want.

How many times have you gone on holiday and checked reviews on Trip Advisor, before you booked? I know I have and I still do all the time.

How many times have you booked a hotel and checked the testimonials before you've booked it? How many times have you gone to a restaurant and checked out what people are saying about that restaurants food or service by Googling them?

It's just normal nowadays and your salon is being checked out as we speak, right now.

What are you saying to your prospective clients? Are you reinforcing your message? Or turning them off?

We're all wanting to know that when we spend our hard earned money with a business that we not only get good value, but we also want to spend good money when we realise that we have a connection with that business.

Having that connection is so paramount to making your business grow with the right clients who are prepared to pay a really good price to come and see you.

So now you've done all the hard work and you've created your posts, you've created the noise that needs to get you attention from prospective clients and they now know you exist, (most salon owners give up at this stage) and they like the fact that you say you can fix their problem. The next thing they are going to do is, they're going to check you out, anyway they can.

You need to know, that all your time, money and energy that you've spent to attract their attention, to get new clients to know you are the one that can help fix their problems, to getting you to be seen as an authority, the number one in their eyes, the expert in town, don't stop there. Now you need to hold their hand and guide them, to prove to them that you are the one.

The fact is only 55% of visitors spend less than 15 seconds on your website. Not very long hey!

You get one shot, to get across to them the message that you want them to see. They are looking for you to prove to them that you are the person that's going to look after their needs. You get this short time to prove to them that you can talk the talk and walk the walk. They're going to check you out to see if you fit into their life, be ready for them, get ready to guide them and make it easy for them to buy, if they are ready today.

It's a terrifying fact that 98% of website visitors never return back to that site. Don't mess this up!

The reason that this is so important, the reason that this is paramount to you now is that your posts and your adverts on Facebook and social media are yesterdays news. They're one flick away from being gone but if you can get them onto your website then your website lives on, your message lives on.

We also want to make sure that you're not working harder at this, you're busy enough, you see your website has all of your messages on it, all of your good stuff, all you have to do is guide them to your website and your website will do all the heavy lifting for you. It keeps your salon top of mind whenever they are ready to change salons.

Most hairdressers and beauticians I know aren't particularly computer savvy. You don't know how to build a website and building a website isn't something that you really want to learn how to do either, it's just not your thing. But what you must understand is that when people come to your website they come because they want more knowledge. They want you to educate them, to help them, to solve a problem.

There tends to be 3 types of people who will come and visit your website.

I like to think of them like traffic lights, Green, Amber and Red.

Green visitors (around 3% are ready to buy now).
Amber visitors (They make up 67% of the people that are curious, but are just not ready yet. They haven't fallen out of love with their current salon yet, but they are looking for another salon, for when the time comes, usually they are giving their salon one last chance). The Amber visitors don't leave their

current salons on a whim.

Red visitors (The remaining 30%. These people are nowhere near ready, they are not even interested and are just taking a sticky beak. But let's not rule them out just yet).

Let's take a look at the Green visitor (3% ready to buy) who come to your website and are ready to buy now.

They're just looking for reassurance and a way to contact you. So what are you going to do with these Green people? Well, maybe you want to direct them to your price list, so that when they call your salon they know exactly how much it's going to cost them, (making sure you are eliminating the bargain chasers) also so they know exactly how long the service is going to take, these people will know exactly what they're asking for, because these clients are ready to buy today.

So make sure you've got a 'book now' on your website, make sure you have got 'your address' on your website and make sure you've got a 'phone number' incase they want to call. So a 'book here' or 'call here' button must be visible because they're ready for action, they're ready to spend their money and they want an appointment now.

The Amber visitor (67% not quite ready, but very interested) are the biggest group of people, you will notice that the biggest group of people that come to your website aren't ready to buy just yet.

These people are always forgotten about as most salon owners want instant gratification, they want results now. So these people are generally neglected and no one really looks after them. Which is crazy, because they are the biggest group of people, with the most money and are the most loyal, as you will see later on!

Most salons tend to only go after the Green visitors, the people that are ready to buy now. Whereas the biggest group of people, the Amber visitor, they're checking you out, but they haven't fallen out with their current salon as yet. Their hairdresser hasn't annoyed them or ignored them enough, their beautician hasn't rushed them through. They just feel a little bit upset and are starting to look for another salon to call home, they are looking for a salon that solves their problem, a common interest and a community.

These Amber visitors are the people that you really want to attract. They should be your number 1 focus. These amber visitors, even though they're not ready to make the move just yet, but the good thing about the Amber people is that when they make their move and they move to a new salon they don't leave on a whim, they don't leave on price, they took a long time to choose you and they'll take a long time to leave you also. As long as you don't annoy them, abuse their trust, or take them for granted they will stay for a very, very long time.

So you need things on your website that are going to help them decide that your salon is the salon that will solve their problems, treat them with respect and deliver on what you promised.

So you need to win them over.

You need proof, maybe have some before and afters, so that they get to see your work.

They may want to see your price menu to see if they can afford you, so guide them to your price menu also. You also might want to write a few blogs to grab their interest.

Blogs are just a few words that you write on your website, a bit like you did when we talked about authority. You work out what problems they need solving and you show and tell them how you can solve it.

Maybe you'll put some case studies in there, some case studies of clients that you've done and how you done it, step by step, how it changed your clients lives, how what you did solved their problem.

You should be getting some of your clients to write testimonials, and show these to the Amber visitors also.

Amber visitors will want to see proof that you can walk the walk, they have come to your website to see if your salon is the one.

This is the time to show off your work, you show your testimonials off, you show off how you can fix their problem, you show them case studies.

You want these Amber visitors, as soon as they visit your website they're going to know that you've built this salon for them, and they're going to be hungry for more information so make sure your website has all the information they will be looking for on it. You don't need to overload them but you do need to think about their problems, what they have come searching for.

So if you're a blonde hair expert you'll definitely have things on the website about how to look after your blonde hair, how to grow your blonde hair, how to make your blonde hair stay blonde for 6 weeks, how to repair damaged blonde hair, etc. If you're the waxing expert you might talk about ingrowing hairs or what sort of wax you use because that's what they're interested in and that's what you're good at and that's what matters to them.

I would always try to get an Amber visitors email address by offering them a 'how to sheet' or a 'how to video' so that I can email them and try to win them over. They may never come back to the website, but I hope to email them proof of what I do and what problems that I fix, but also keep me front of mind for when they are ready to move salons.

We then are left with the Red visitor (the 30% that's left, the reds, they're coming just to check you out, they are not interested in moving salons). They are still in love with their salon at the moment and have no intention of moving at all. The die hards! But all clients were once die hard fans and eventually they do move salons, and I want you to be ready.

It's almost impossible to get a Red visitor to call and book in your salon, they have no intention of leaving their current salon, they are just looking because a post, or ad, or a friend might have mentioned you. But don't give up on these visitors, not just yet!

So what do you do with a Red visitor? You try and turn them into an Amber visitor.

So again just like the amber visitor you may want to direct them to your before and afters, and all the stuff that you have added to your website to win over an Amber visitor. It's a really good idea at this stage and especially for the Red visitor, to get their email address off them and hopefully you can email them more proof, and really interesting 'how to's', so they start to fall in love with you or at least become an amber, and feel that their current salon is just not cutting it any more.

They may start to feel that their salon isn't quite up to your standard and a chink in their armour may happen, and then eventually they'll start to feel a little bit niggled towards their current salon, if they are being taken for granted and then they'll start to turn into Amber.

And if you talk to them enough, send them enough interesting emails and direct them back to your blogs, so they suck some more of your information, they might even turn to Green.

If we are thinking that there are 3 types of visitors who arrive at your website, you need to have the 3 elements on your website. Green visitor, they're ready to act. If they're Amber you turn them into a Green. If they're Red you turn them into an Amber and then turn them into a Green.

That's why you get your website, your Facebook page, your Google presence, to drive people into your salon. The majority of salon owners don't do this and don't take this seriously enough, which means, they do all the advertising and they find out that it doesn't work. They try posts and say it doesn't work. They give up because what they do isn't working and they say that, "clients only want specials", well they're just missing the next step out, and the next step is quite simple, they don't realise that the majority of people that visit their website or Facebook page aren't ready yet, they expect instant return on the post or advert. But that's not the way it works now, things have changed. They just haven't changed to Green yet.

Now remember the Amber visitors and the Red visitors aren't quite ready to buy from you today but we know one day they will start looking? You need to keep front of mind with these visitors and a great way to do this is to follow them all over the Facebook newsfeed (what did he just say that I can follow people who have visited my website all over Facebook?) Well, yes you can!

The clever people at Facebook have come up with a Pixel (a code) you can just copy and paste that pixel into the backend of your website and if you don't know how to do this maybe ask your website techie guy and he'll do it for you.

Once the pixel is on your website, you go back to Facebook ads manager and create an audience (call it everyone that visited my website), and Facebook collects everyones details who lands on your website and stores it under your audience. Clever hey!

You can then create an advert about their problems, and how you have a solution and you can advertise that to only these people. It will pop up in their newsfeed so they'll see you everywhere, and you will always be on their mind. Now that's pure genius!

Have you ever been on a website looking for a pair of shoes, a dress or a watch and then the next time you're on Facebook all you keep seeing are watches and dresses and shoes all over the place, well that's because they have a Facebook pixel and have created an audience, so they can retarget you. Now that's what you do too, to all the Amber and Red visitors because you know they've come to your website, you know they're keen to look for another salon otherwise they wouldn't be there, but they're just not convinced yet. Then you get to put your message in front of them, every day, letting them know you are an authority, the problems that they want solving, your salon is the best salon to fix it.

Your aim is to win them over, keep your salon front of mind in their newsfeed and then they fall in love with you and you turn them into Green visitors.

Your website is a living breathing information hub that tells the world what you do and who you serve.

Keeping it updated with blogs, videos and 'how to's', and some case studies, it makes sense to direct some of your posts and traffic's attention away from Facebook and onto your website, you never know when Facebook will change the way that they operate.

With more visitors reaching your website it will lift your website ranking up in Google, and get you found quicker, for all the people who to want check you out or Google a problem that they have, it will be easier for them to find you if your website is fully loaded with stuff that they search for.

For example when I had my salon if someone ever typed in curly hair expert I was ranked number one in Google because I had video's, testimonials, blogs and 'how to' care for curly hair all over my website. So Google pushed me up to number one.

Also if they'd Googled 'Award winning hair salon' I'd won enough awards and I talked about it in my blogs, it got me ranked up there pretty quickly, so that when people typed in 'award winning hair salon in

Erina' which is where my salon was, I would of course come up as number one, I worked hard to be the number one spot, that gave me free advertising to a lot of people as most people with a problem will Google that problem first.

As a salon owner it's your responsibility to make sure that all your posts and adverts are seen by the correct people, then take them on an intangible journey to 'win them over'.

To help you choose which platform (Facebook, Google Instagram, etc) you should be spending more time on and your hard earned money, is to ask your clients how they found you. That's the minimum you should be expected to do, ask every single brand new client that comes through your door how they heard about you and why they chose you above other salons.

I did this for 15 years as a salon owner and it is one of the first things I recommend to all of my salon clients. It's the fastest and best way to get feed back on your marketing. Why they chose you, what blogs are working and what posts are working and of course what's not. But more importantly how they found you, because that's where you will concentrate more of your efforts. If most Google you then that's where you should spend your time, effort and money making your webpage and Google presence bigger and better. If most prospects are coming from Facebook, then maybe you should spend more time, more money or more adverts on Facebook.

Being smart with your marketing money means you spend less and get more clients as a result.

As a coach I still ask my clients how they found me, because I need to know also where I need to spend my time, energy and money just like you do.

CASE STUDY

Being 24 years of age and opening my own business almost 2 years ago Richard and his support has helped me reach every dream I have set yet!

To me Richard from I salon coaching is a constant support when you don't know who else to ask. You can tell he is passionate about what he is teaching and has really lived our life before. Trust me I worked for Richard in salon for almost 5 years and I have now been officially Coached by him for 1 year. In and out of the salon I have never doubted his passion for successful hairdressing salons. Within my first year of business Richard has helped me get an outstanding 210% growth from 2016-2017. We together have set a 30% growth goal for this year and I feel privileged to have him along side to support my goals.

To say the least this course has changed my life and my perception of my future. My goal is to own a salon I don't need to work in whilst maintaining a wonderful wage packet. I will not stop until I reach that goal. Because thanks to Richard I can see that dream as a reality.

Tamara Beal, Meraki Hair Creations, NSW, Australia

Core Story

With the evolution and popularity of social media it's become easier and easier to connect with like minded people all around the world. We're so used to connecting with like minded people that when someone goes and chooses a new hair salon or beauty salon they want to connect with like minded people also. If they cannot find a connection with you, they will keep looking until they find a salon owner that they do have a connection with.

So it has never, ever before been more apparent that people buy from people they like.

They need to know you, they need to know things about you, they need to trust you and they need to believe in you.

More and more people are choosing to buy from people they like.

If you're in business then you're in the people business because business is people and takings are the numbers.

On average 67% of the people in your town are checking you and your salon out right now, to see if you are the sort of person that they want to do business with, that they want to connect with, and if they like you?

They are searching and they are looking for you right now whilst you are reading this book.

Potential clients and potential staff want to belong to something bigger than themselves, a tribe you might call it, a movement. They are looking for something and someone that they can connect with, a community of like minded people.

It used to be said that most businesses needed a 'visions statement', 'a mission statement' or a 'unique selling point' to set them apart from everyone else. So that clients could tell the difference between the businesses.

That was the old way, you still need to set yourself apart from everybody else, but with social media being a part of every day life, they have become accustomed to a more personal connection, so it's you that they are interested in and whether you are the one that can solve their problem.

And if they walk into your salon, do they feel comfortable, like it's home, do they feel confident that you've built the salon just for them, so they feel safe and surrounded by like minded people.

Core story is made up of these simple core elements that will set your salon apart and move you way above anybody else.

The Old Way: You needed a USP, a unique selling point.
The New Way: Your Core Story.

Today I'm going to share with you how to build your very own core story, and why it's so important that you have one. You will share this core story on your website, Facebook, leaflets, adverts, job adverts, business cards and anything and everything that you do.

Get your core story correct and your prospective clients will believe in you, will feel they belong to your salon and if people believe your core story they will stay more loyal to your salon, to the core, to you, because you cannot only fix their problem and you built the salon for them, but they will feel content that when they walk in your salon it feels like home.

This is also useful, because when you lose a staff member most of the clients will stay loyal to your brand, to you because it's your salon that attracted them, not the staff member. If the staff member leaves to open their own salon, they may try to replicate your core story and try to convince your clients to come to them. But it's your core story and it has come from inside you, from the heart, it's hard to replicate and stay true, clients will know if someone is just trying to copy someone else and not be real.

Many years ago people were loyal to certain brands, but with discount sites like Groupon, and salon owners trying to get clients in with discounts and specials, they have accustomed clients to shop around and grab a bargain, they have encouraged clients not to be loyal.

But now loyalty is stronger than ever, but it's stronger in community's, to belong to something, to you, to your core story.

You're doing life with these people and people are now choosing who they do life with.

Price is not the deciding factor for people that want to connect to you through your core story. But they need to know that you're different from the others, they need to get you, to truly understand you, and you need to get them. So they can decide if your salon is the salon they want to do business with. They will not choose you on price, so no need to do discounts to get them in. But don't be bland or average, be true to you.

Remember birds of a feather still flock together.

That means these people are looking for a connection with you. If you get to attract the right person to your salon, you can do your best work on them. It's a win, win.

You get to filter out the people that you don't want, and attract the people that you do want. To attract the right clients and to repel the wrong ones as you know they are not for you and they too know you are not for them.

Think about this scenario for a moment. Your salon is an organic salon and you strongly believe that you want to save the planet, so you've gone plastic free. If that's something that really is true to you, to your core and you live by that, when you open your salon door is that what the prospective client sees? If that is the truth, then people will believe you, and you'll attract people that also believe in the same ethics, who wouldn't want to go to a salon that is environmentally friendly, go to a salon that's thinking of the worlds health first, or a salon that's thinking about not putting nasty toxins in the air or down the drain. If prospective clients also lived with the same ethics they would love your salon, so they can sit and have their hair done in peace or sit and have their nails done without the smell of strong chemicals giving them headaches.

They would truly feel that they belonged in your salon and it was built especially for people like them.

You see whatever your core story is, everyone has a different core story, it means that you're unique, that your staff can't leave you and take that core story with them because they're not true to that story, only you are.

By using your core story it's really important that when you tell the world about your story you are attracting similar people, who love you for what you do and who you are. It makes your work day so much better. It means attracting clients who also have exactly the same outlook in life, and staff that come and work for you, they could never leave you and work down the road because they love everything about you.

It makes it so much easier to attract clients and attract staff to your salon.

Let's dive in and find out what makes up a Core Story?

Your Core story is made of 3 important elements that make up your salon culture:

All About

All about You
All about Them
All about Us

We start off on the top left hand side with You.

Your why.

What gets you out of bed in the morning?
Why do you have a salon?
Why did you leave your old salon?
What's important to you salon wise and home wise?
What are your ethics?
Who do like being around?
Who do you do your best work with?
What are your salons dreams?

Where are you trying to take your salon?
What would it look like when it's completed?
What would it smell like?
What will the colours be?
What type of decor, music and values will the salon have?
What type of client will be there sitting in the salon?

We use this to build your salons foundations, your dream salon. How big do you want your salon to be, how many staff, what type of clients do you want to do, what would you love to do and your salon ethos? This way staff and clients in your salon are happy, they share some of your thoughts and know you've built the salon for them. Share your story to whoever will listen, people will know what you're about as everyone is a potential client or potential staff member.

Let's take a look at these two hypothetical hair salons, both have different ethos and are both aiming at different clients.

You can see straight away that both salon owners have different dreams for their salons.

Beauty-Do Hair Salon sits in a shopping complex.

A brightly painted sign at the front of the shop states the salon name and that they offer just hair cuts. Through large plate glass windows, you can watch the team of stylists cutting hair.

When you walk in the front door, one of the stylists greets you and tells you to have a seat — someone will be with you in a second.

You head over to the waiting area which is mostly white with bright colours for accent. You sit in a white plastic patio chair, and you see a magazine rack overflowing with six months worth of gossip mags. As you look around the salon, you notice it is buzzing with activity. Not only are people working, but they are also gossiping amongst themselves. The local radio station is blaring in the background. The stylists are wearing casual clothes and all seem very chatty.

Panache Hair Salon is located about five minutes away, close to an office park.

It has its own private parking, and the front of the shop has a modest sign in muted colours. Frosting covers most of the windows. You walk through the front door into a reception area that looks like it belongs in a 'Home Beautiful' design magazine and you notice a light scent of fresh flowers.

The receptionist, dressed stylishly, greets you professionally and personally escorts you to the waiting area. The waiting area has elegant watercolour paintings on the walls and large comfortable sofas. The receptionist informs you that you will have a short wait and inquires if you would like some tea or mineral water. You sit back and listen to the classical music playing in the background. You see the stylists in their spotless clothes quietly going about their work.

If you come in off the street and know absolutely nothing about these two salons, what are your impressions and expectations?

What type of customer will each salon attract?

They both have different goals and that is based on the salon owners dream, what they want their salon to be like.

And that gives prospective clients and staff a way to select the business which best suits their needs.

Knowing your 'why', and 'your clients problems', this enables your salon to provide it deliberately by building a salon culture targeted to those customers' needs.

That's what your Core Story is all about — describing the feelings you want your customer to have as they experience your salon.

Your prospective clients don't need to visit your physical location in order to receive your core story from your salon. Every time your clients or prospective clients visit your Web site, receive a brochure via mail or e-mail, call you on the phone, meet with a staff member, or interact with your salon in any way, they are receiving your core story.

When I opened up my first salon in Australia I was new, I was a migrant, I had no clients, no one had heard of me at all, I knew no one. I had just bought a salon and did a massive refit, scared, but I had a dream where I wanted to take my salon. I knew which direction I was heading and I knew how to get there. I wanted to have the best salon in town, employing the best trained people, paying my staff the best money. I wanted the best clients, clients who paid the best money, that visited me more often. I told everybody this, anyone who would dare to listen. I advertised for staff telling them this in the advert and in person, "I'm going to have the best salon in town", if you want to come and work for the best, I'll train you to be the best, it's going to be hard work but I'll get you there".

Everybody knew what my Core Story was, everybody knew my 'Why', everybody knew why I was setting up this salon and who I wanted to attract, and they came in truck loads, because they knew I had built the salon for them. Staff and clients, they both came in truckloads. I had an abundance of them and very, very quickly I grew my salon very, very fast.

Don't underestimate the power of sharing your dream!

Your 'Why' is very, very important to everyone. It can be about your salon or it can be personal but what matters to you, matters to them.

Let's take a look at the right hand side circle next, All About Them

This is where we talk about the clients problems, we've done this before in the authority chapter.

If you haven't already, make a list of all the clients problems that you love to fix, do it now.

Curly hair
Blonde hair
Clients complaining about waiting too long
Clients being taken for granted

This list can be as long as you want, and you also must enjoy fixing these problems.

I loved cutting curly hair, so curly hair was my thing.

Remember these clients are looking for a salon to fix their problems, so you need to be able to talk about them in depth. That's what being the Authority, the expert is all about. If clients feel you are the expert they will seek you out and be ready to let you take care of them. This part of your Core Story you will use to back up your claims of being an expert.

If you talk a lot about curly haired people you've got to love doing curly hair, you've got to love to fix it. It has to be part of your ethos, you've got to love to do that, pretty simple. People go to the doctors to fix a problem, you have to be like the doctor, know their problems and have the solution.

Let's take a look at the bottom circle now, All About Us. Your Salon Culture.

Imagine you have allergic reactions to dairy and wheat, it's something you've always had and it's so annoying because you cannot find a coffee shop anywhere to get your daily dose of caffeine, so you have this brain wave to open one up yourself.

Your coffee shop will be different from others around because you're going to sell gluten free treats, raw treats with unrefined sugar, you're going to play very soft music that's all about balancing the body and mind, and relaxation, the coffee's going to be fair trade, the milks are going to be sourced from activated organic nuts. You're going to offer almond milk, coconut milk and macadamia milk. You have built this coffee shop because it's your world and you feel others must feel the same, people that care about the environment and their health, for people that want dairy and wheat free.

Now people who are like you and are interested in having food and drinks that are dairy and wheat free are going to come to your coffee shop because they believe you. As soon as they walk through the door they'll know that you built this coffee shop just for them, to solve their problems, if they have allergies to dairy or if they only want coffee that's fair trade, then yours is the coffee shop that answers all of their prayers.

If you've really built this coffee shop for these types of people, when they come in they need to know that you live and breathe this sort of life for them. They'll get why you're doing it, your why will stand out, they'll get that you are solving their problems, that they're allergic to dairy or wheat so they don't want to have dairy or wheat anywhere in the shop, they know that you're taking their problems seriously.

And if you over deliver, they will be really impressed and you will have a client for life, what about homemade almond milk or activated nuts or homemade macadamia milk, they'll go nuts for that (pun intended), because they'll know you live and breathe their world.

But if you start weakening your story and what I mean by weakening your story is, if you imagine you're now going to sell sweets and lollies for the kids, that are full of sugar or hot chocolate that's not ethically sourced but rather just bought from the local supermarket. If this starts to happen people will start to feel that you don't really care. If other people start to come to the coffee shop and you start altering the menu to please them also, so going against your core values, the tribe of people that you set this shop up for are going to feel neglected or that you haven't built this for them after all, and they'll start dropping off, start looking for another coffee shop to call home.

Because they wont believe your story anymore. You must not abuse their trust.

Looking at your salon now, are you living your why? What needs to change to back up your why and your clients problems?

I want to share a story about a client of mine, a hair salon owner. Her salon is aiming at clients that want low toxins in the products that she uses, she doesn't like chemicals and she's all about saving the planet.

I would visit her salon because I too live that life. And I don't want chemicals in the air while I have my hair cut.

But she's also doing a smoothing service in her salon, that has formaldehyde in it!

Now to me if I went to her salon and I believed her story to get me there, and I sat there next to a client who was having this smoothing service done and I knew there was formaldehyde in it, I would never go back, in fact I would tell all my friends not to go there too. I would know she was fake, I would know she's wrong, I would know she doesn't truly believe in low toxins and I would then feel a disconnection between us. You see how important it is to live what you say you do, why your core story is so important to you?

We need complete transparency for all, a clear picture. We need to feel that connection.

Get your salon culture right and everyone knows where you stand, and what you care about. Everyone knows who you're there to serve, everyone knows that the whole salon believes this too, your team are on the same page as you, you are all telling the same story. You know if you opened a salon that is ethical then your coffee has to be that way, you'll deal with the hair on the floor in a certain way, you'll deal with your towels in a certain way. Everything you do will live and breathe what you're about.

Because it really makes sense to actually live the life that you're meant to live.

You're following your destiny.

And because you've also got other people in the world you're not the only person that believes this. Other people are looking for salons like yours and what a great community to build together.

How great is it to belong! It's all about belonging.

You want to make your salon the destination and 'you' the core story of the salon destination.

Clients will feel at home in your salon. They will feel your 'why'. They will feel everything about you as they open the door, the music, the smell of the coffee, the candles, the atmosphere.

Your team will feel it also, and your salon lives and breathes your 'why'.

With the hair and beauty industry going through the biggest scarcity of staff that the salon world has ever seen, you need to have a connection with them too.

We have statistics that say 40% of staff are thinking about leaving you right now. That's almost half of your workforce who are thinking of leaving. If they lived and breathed your culture, if they too loved everything about your 'why' then they too will feel that the salon was built for them. Why would they leave, it's their dream salon!

So if you can attract the right staff to your salon, that believe your 'why' and want to live in that world also, it's very rare that they're actually going to leave you for a salon down the road that they have no connection with whatsoever. It's not all about the money anymore. It's about community and belonging. To being part of something bigger. Get this right and your staff worries could be a thing of the past.

If you want to see a great example of 'why' check out Simon Sinek he has a great book called, 'It Starts With Why', he also has a great Ted talk on this.

People need to know your why.

Gary Vaynerchuk calls it, 'The North Star'. When things get tough, when things get hard if you know your North Star, your 'why', it'll keep you going in the right direction when things go wrong.

It keeps you moving forward to get your salon to where you want it to be, regardless of how frantic your months become.

How a good core story will stop you in your tracks.

While I was away doing one of my seminars in Mackay (a small mining town in Queensland) my wife and I wanted to go out to eat for dinner. Now never having been to Mackay before we did what most people do and that's Google restaurants in the area. We were looking for an Indian restaurant and there were approximately 15 Indian restaurants in town. But as soon as I saw this particular Indian restaurants website, I stopped looking immediately and booked a table right away. I didn't even carry on looking at the rest of them.

What stopped me looking at them all?

What made me decide to choose this particular restaurant?

Well, it wasn't price (this restaurant we later found out was the most expensive in town). It wasn't the food, I hadn't even seen the menu and it wasn't the reviews.

It was their core story, that made me book a table straight away, I just had to go and experience the restaurant.

Their restaurant is called Roshni and they explain on their website what it means....

"Roshni stands for happiness and light, contemporary designed and influenced by ancient Indian traditions, Roshni offers a sophisticated dining and takeaway experience. With its intoxicating mix of old and new setting, its effortlessly charming staff and its tantalising food will make you want to come back for more.

Their website opens with this message

' A fine Indian cuisine, we create delicious memories'

Their story goes like this.......

'Roshni is the creation of two people Raj a Restauranteur from Brisbane and Jessica a marketing professional from Mackay. Raj and Jess' story starts with the couple meeting by chance in a Brisbane conference which then followed into a true love story not just with each other but with their creation of Roshni followed by their creation of their beautiful baby daughter Lily.

Their mission, Roshnis' mission has always been about providing exceptional food and service to our customers whilst utilising Mackay and the surrounding regions fresh produce. Supporting and helping our community through good times and tough times, and putting our hand up to help whenever and wherever we are able.

This story of their 'why' they opened their restaurant and who they want to visit blew me away. I believed them and booked there and then, I wanted to be part of their journey.

And I wasn't disappointed, the food was exquisite and service was second to none.

If you are ever in Mackay, go visit them. And to top off the night, on the way home from the restaurant the owner sent me a personal text message thanking me for my custom. I never even got to meet him. It's all part of the service they do.

If I lived in Mackay they would have a customer for life. They have the best core story I hope you agree and see how a core story can take a prospective client, to an actual client that is so excited to be part of your journey.

And the price had never even entered my head. It's all about believing that your salon is made for them.

I want to close the Core Story with a really important analogy.

Imagine that your success, your why is at the top of a huge mountain. And when you have finished your journey and you get to the summit you can breathe and say, "I made it, my salon is exactly what I envisioned, I have the amount staff that I thought I would have, the number of clients, a good amount of money coming in, the life I always wanted to live, I have got more purpose in life now, more freedom, it has given me more money, I have made it".

As you take the steps up that mountain to success and you have shared your core story of how big the mountain is with your team, you and they are going to embark on this journey together.

When you share your 'why' your big picture ideal with your team they then have two choices to make.

1. They help take some of the load, they will help carry you and lift some of the heavy load up that mountain, they're with you 110% all the way, they believe in you and they're backing you and they've got your back.
2. They don't like your story, they don't care about your story, they just care about themselves, they don't even care about the salon culture, and you're going to be dragging them up that mountain all the way to the top.

And eventually you're going to have to decide, do you want to drag them all the way to the top kicking and screaming or are you going to cut them loose?

And the good thing is, they get to choose not you, they make the decision. You tell them your big picture story, where you're going, what your salon's about, what you're about, who you're trying to fix and they're either going to come along and belong to your salon or it's just going to be a job and you're going to drag them all the way.

The decision is theirs, you just have to be big enough to act on that decision.

CASE STUDY

I have to say that all of the modules are pretty amazing.. all in all it gave me clarity and focused direction. It helps to keep me on task and on targets as it can sometimes be overwhelming with so many hats to wear as an owner and mentor. Little bites, time and pressure, slow and steady wins the race. Richard breaks down this course in a very simple understandable way that in the end makes the big picture stand out in the brightest of colours.. all we have to do is follow direction and complete each task at hand. The helping hand is at the end of my own sleeve.. he has made me more compelled to use that hand, with accountability.

I repeat these modules over and over again. This knowledge is definitely the power. Thank you so much Richard!

Tammy Coyston, Wikhead Hair, Canada

Keep In Touch

In a perfect world your prospective client would see your post or your advert and call your salon immediately, demanding that you book them in. Begging and pleading with you to let them have an appointment, with any employee in your salon, and they'll pay you whatever it costs to get themselves booked in ASAP. They arrive at your salon and they love you straight away and they beg you to let them rebook for the next 6 weeks, in fact for the whole of the year. They ask to be booked in on your quietest days because they don't want to take up your busy days, they know that you're busy and they are happy to oblige and help you in any way they can.

They leave your salon arms full with bags of retail and big a smiley face, heading off to tell all of their friends and anyone else they know, to go to your salon because the salon is fantastic and amazing.

But we don't live in a perfect world!

That means you need to be one step ahead of your clients, you need to take control and look at how you can fill those quiet days, get the clients spending more and spreading the word about your salon.

You need to be more savvy.

Every salon that I take on as a coaching client is leaking money and I'm sure your salon is leaking money too. I'm talking bucket loads of money.

If your salon was a bucket it would be full of holes, leaking money out, no matter how much liquid you put in there it will never fill to the top. Not unless you start to fill some of those holes.

In this chapter 'Keep in Touch', you will learn how to fill some of those holes and save your salon thousands of dollars every year.

There is no other way to describe this loss than using percentages, and I hope that I will be able to help you understand how important these numbers are. I know maths may not be your strong point, but bear with me, this will be worth it. I promise.

No matter how much water you add into your bucket (your salon) it's just never going to fill to the brim with all those holes!

Let's look at some of those holes that are leaking money and learn how to plug them FAST.

Two of the main category's that your salon is leaking money are:

1. New clients

2. Existing clients

Let's take a look how you can keep in touch with your clients and start plugging those holes.

New clients

Looking at the new clients that are visiting your salon.

New client retention is very low for most salons.

Believe it or not, a good performing salon is only keeping on average 20% of all its new clients that walk in their doors.

That's about two clients out of every ten new clients that they will get to keep as regulars.

You're leaking from your bucket on average 8 new clients in your salon. That's something that needs addressing don't you think?

There is no point in you spending all of your money attracting new clients to your salon if you just lose most of them after their first visit.

That figure can be a lot higher with salons that have strategies in place to ensure they keep their new clients coming back.

I want your salon to be great, I want to take your salon from good to great.

A great salon is keeping on average up to 50% of all the new clients that enter their salon doors.

That means 5 clients out of 10 clients will return with a great salon.

That's a 150% increase in client retention.

If your salon is currently running at 50% new client retention then your salon is doing great, but let's do even better.

Existing clients

Every salon will be losing some of their regular clients every single week, and your clients are no exception, they are dropping off and I want to help you plug that hole right now today, well, at least fill it as best as you can.

The average salon loses around 28% of it's existing clientele every year.

That equates to 28% of your salons turnover walking out of your door and heading into your competitors salon.

Astonishing isn't it?

Yep, you are losing 28% of your clients right now, they are leaving you, to never return!

I wanted to repeat that because this is very important to your salons growth.

You might not be realising or feeling it now, but if you stopped attracting new clients to your salon, and your regular salon clients are decreasing, your takings will eventually drop and you will start to struggle to pay your bills. This might be happening to you right now?

So you see it's really, really important that you keep in touch with your clients.

If your client is not rebooked back in your salon you MUST keep in touch with them at all times.

We live in a busy world and everybody is busy, including your clients. They live in a busy world just like you do .

They are all really busy people, they have school runs to do, kids to take to sports after school, shopping and general running around doing their usual work. They have their stresses from work too that they've got to deal with and the last thing they think about is looking after themselves.

Eventually they will stop and get two minutes for a breather, but they might think that you're too busy to squeeze them in. Or they leave it too long between their last visit and they just forget how long it's been and that they're overdue, then they may even resort to popping into another salon as they're passing because it's convenient.

You want to take the responsibility away from them and get the client rebooked back in, but if they cannot for any reason then you will want to encourage, remind, and tempt them back into the salon at all times. You will want to be front of their mind for when they are ready.

With the average salon retention of existing clients being around 72% that means your salon is losing 28% of its turnover per year.

Let me repeat that because this is so important. In fact stop reading right now and find how much your salons annual takings are! Now pop that number into a calculator and x by 28%. That figure you are looking at right now is how much your salon is losing (leaking hole) every year.

Scary isn't it? That's why most salons stay in the War Zone, it's money that's leaking out of their salons that they didn't know was missing. But now you do!

Clients simply leave you because they have no commitment from you. Think about every new client you get, every walk in client is a loss for another salon.

Your clients are no different, they are the same.

So if your salon generally looks after 100 clients a week then 28 of them are not coming back.

I hope these numbers have got your attention, because your salon, every salon is losing money, leaking money from the holes in their bucket (salon)

Using the strategy 'Keep In Touch' you can have a massive impact on your salons takings without even attracting any new clients.

This single strategy can save your salon thousands and thousands of dollars every year.

Most salons today are computerised and use pretty good salon software to keep track of their takings, clients and staff.

That computer and software cost you a lot of money and most salon owners just tend to use it as an expensive till. Really it's a gold mine and there's gold in them there hills.

Your software system has all the information that you need to plan a strategy to keep more of your new clients and it also has the capability of plugging some of those holes to stop you losing your existing clients. Use your database to internally get some of the money back that you are losing, to grow your salon.

If you can 'Keep In Touch' with your clients, you can let them know why they came to you in the first place, share stories and keep you front of mind.

You can also use this strategy to get your existing clients to visit sooner and super boost your revenue.

Take a look at this example, this is what happened in my salon a few years ago.

I always track the average visits of my clients. My average visits between appointments was 8.2 weeks. Then the big recession happened and gaps started to appear in my appointment book.

I knew my client retention hadn't changed, but gaps were still appearing. I checked my client visits and soon realised it was now at 9.2 weeks between appointments. The clients were starting to stretch their appointments out.

By just one week, that's all! Not much difference you might think.

That one week made a huge difference to my takings, if I had done nothing I would have lost around $100,000 per year. That's how much this would impact my salon and of course your salon too.

So I went into hyperactive mode and used my data base to encourage more clients to return sooner, offering them discounts, bribes to get them in at any cost, and also I had to start attracting more new clients to the salon to fill the holes left after clients started to drag out their appointments.

Sometimes you will need to encourage your clients to visit you sooner, you cannot control recessions or other outside factors that effect the economy, but you can affect your clients buying thoughts.

You could use a text message or send an email (costs nothing it's free) with a little something that says, "Come and get your hair done".

I have been doing this strategy for 25 years, first I started it manually, before we had a computer system, good old fashioned pen and paper. But when I got computerised it made my life a whole lot easier.

If you weren't rebooked in my salon I would send you an email when 8 weeks had lapsed.

I would also send you an email if you hadn't returned by week 10.

If you still hadn't responded to either email or text, you would get another little nudge by week 12.

If you still hadn't returned I would send another message out at week 25, usually with a survey, to find out why you hadn't been back, because something has obviously gone wrong.

And if you still hadn't returned by week 52, I would send you an amnesty to come and visit the salon for free.

I felt that it was that important to me to keep every client I could.

You may be thinking,"I cannot believe you are a business coach, and recommending discounting of our services". Yes, I believe discounting is good for your business when used correctly.

I also hear many salon owners say this, and you might be the same, "If I send emails or texts to my clients offering discounts to come in, they're just going to wait for those discounts because it's going to be cheaper, and then they will never pay full price".

Yes, some might, but either they can't afford you or they need encouragement to come in. It's better than losing them altogether.

What matters is that they loved your 'Core Story' once, they may still love you now, but maybe they just can't afford you, maybe their lives have changed and something else is more important to them and has priority with their money.

But think about this, if you know they love you but they cannot afford your full price, they will have to leave you for a cheaper salon or only visit you once or twice a year.

But if you know that offering them a discount makes them visit sooner, that gives you the power to say, 'When they can come in', and 'who they can be booked with' and 'for how much you will charge them'.

It's a win, win. You get to keep your clients, you get to direct the client to your quiet days and with your quietest employee. The alternative is losing that client, keeping your quieter staff quiet, and your slower days slow. I know what I'd rather be doing.

You don't always have to give discounts to get clients to come in.

> I used different methods depending on what results I wanted. Here are a few:
> I built loyalty with my emails because I reminded my clients about my 'Core Story' with every email that I sent out.
> I done package deals, because I wanted to use my slow services with my main services and double up.
> I done discounted deals, because when I discounted I wanted a fast response, I wanted to fill the same day cancellations or tomorrows unfilled appointments.

I value added some emails, because I wanted to get a client to use a particular stylist that was new to me or new to the floor if they had just finished their apprenticeship.

I was in control, not them and I managed to direct the clients to wherever I needed them.

A returning client spends 33% more than a brand spanking new client. So why would you not spend some of your time keeping your current clients happy.

Clients need to feel wanted, to belong and it's never been more important in todays salon world to build a community for your clients, and to me sending emails or texts and talking to your clients is like sowing your seeds, so you can grow your clients and grow the community. Remember they loved your 'Core Story' once, they love coming to your salon. You can reuse that 'Core Story' with texts and newsletters to remind them about your salon culture and why they first fell in love with you.

Using discounts and offers to get your staff fully booked.

I love a bargain, I bet you do too? Well, that's the same as your clients, we all love saving money, so I use discounts and special offers in my salon to fill quiet staff members on the quiet days.

You see I have always bred my own staff, which means that I took on apprentices and I trained them my way. As they got to year two of their apprenticeship they started to need their own clients.

Too many salon owners leave it too long before they think about clients for their apprentices. If you wait till year three and then let them loose on the salon floor it will take over a year to get them booked up, and your salons wage bill is so high, and this really starts affecting the salon owners profits.

It takes such a long time to build a clientele, around a year or two. But if I had clients out there that loved to come to my salon, that loved me, but couldn't afford me, but still wanted to come to my salon I would use them, wouldn't you?

As a side note, many trainee's or apprentices as they near the end of their training and they are about to graduate to the role of stylist or therapist, there is a growing trend that so many are scared and have a lack of low self esteem. I see it so often with my salon owner clients. These trainees seem to think they are NOT worth the big dollars and it freaks them out. In fact many quit their jobs because of it. So by getting discounted people in their chair makes them feel that they can do the job in hand better and also build their self esteem that we all know they need.

Anyhow what staff member wants to sit around and do nothing all day, only doing 1 or 2 clients per week it's frustrating for them and the owner, so why do we do it?

Especially so with the scary statistics of salon staff retention. You need to do your bit to keep staff motivated and believing that you are interested in them. And that means getting them doing what they are employed to do. Look after clients.

The client would benefit because they get to visit the salon they love, but at the moment may be just out of their reach financially.

My staff member benefits because they get to do clients that comes to them instead of coming to me or my more experienced staff, and start to build up their own clientele, they don't feel useless and start to build up their self esteem because clients are coming to them and they are doing what they are trained to do.

It's a win for you. You get your quiet days busy and booked out. You get trainee staff or quiet staff busy making you money. You get clients visiting more often, and you have seen how much that can affect your takings. And you also get to fill those leaking holes, stop losing clients.

It's a win, win for everybody.

We all love a great bargain

If you think, 'keeping in touch' is all about discounts you are wrong, it's bigger than that.

You are building loyalty and friendships and letting clients know that they belong to you and that you are not taking them for granted.

Picture your favourite restaurant and they send you a text message today with money off, or a 2 for 1, or a happy birthday message.

It may say something like this, "Hey Tracey we'd love to help you celebrate your birthday, visit us this month with a friend and your meal is on us, t & c's apply".

Would you go?

I would for sure and if I didn't go I'd be thinking nice things about them, thinking why did I not visit them sooner, what nice people.

Would you feel that they care about you?

You see it's good to give back, it really is.

Some clients may have just forgotten about you, they're busy remember and when they come back in they'll remember the joy and the experience they had when they first visited your salon.

Your number one role, of course, is to get them to rebook back in and get them off your email list, especially your discount email list.

If you know they can afford you and they're just forgetting about you because they're just too busy, then your job is to organise them and take control, we talked about this before. They just forget about you, make them fall in love with you all over again.

Don't underestimate how important keeping in touch with your clients is, always try to send newsletters out regularly connecting your clients to your core story all over again.

You can write about what's happening with fashion, who's wearing what.

It's your authority building stuff here guys.

You get to show off your skills and you get them to keep loving you.

CONVERT

It's community building.

You can send them case studies, thank new clients for visiting you, or a welcome letter and explain your core story to them.

Imagine if you went into a business and the owner sent you a personal text thanking you for your custom. Just like that restaurant owner did for me in Mackay, something as simple as sending a text, but that's all it takes, people want to feel that they are important, that they belong.

I felt that I belonged to his restaurant because he thanked me, how good's that, the feeling was amazing.

I would love to share a campaign I did in my salon to fill a quiet day.

I really struggled in my salon to fill a Wednesday, it was the quietest day of the week and nobody wanted to come on a Wednesday and have their hair done.

So I created what I called 'Wicked Wednesday'. We decided that clients could have a half price colour with a full priced cut and blow dry if they came in on a Wednesday.

I sent out the newsletter to my whole database telling them about this, and within weeks my Wednesdays became booked out, in fact my Wednesdays became so popular that they were booked out for a year in advance.

Yes, some of my regular clients decided to use this offer, because I sent it out to everybody in the system, some moved from a Friday or a Saturday so they could get it cheaper. But that didn't bother me, because I can fill a Friday or a Saturday twice over. So many clients want the busier days. So I was happy, my Wednesdays became one of my top midweek days, and the clients who came in on a Wednesday were happy as they were saving money.

I filled Friday and Saturday very quickly and I now have more clients visiting our salon every week, than ever before, from something as simple as that.

I used my expensive computer till to make me more money. That's what they are there for. I used my software to stop my leaking bucket.

Your bucket is leaking too.

Your salon could be losing 28% of your existing clients as we speak, 28% that's almost a third of your clients.

That's 28% less takings that you are losing over a year. Or looking at this another way is, if you take action and 'Keep In Touch' with your clients you could increase your salons takings by 28% this year without new clients.

This isn't peanuts were talking about here, this is big money.

So today, why don't you start building up your email and text templates ready to go.

If you don't know how to set this up in your salon contact the supplier of your software company and they should be able to set that up for you. It's not that hard I've been doing it for 25 years, even manually.

Good luck.

BTW we teach our salon clients how to do this in our Lifestyle Salon Systems and it's easy money.

So go fill those holes in your bucket and work smarter.

CASE STUDY

Richard, has helped me through some difficult times. He genuinely cares about you as a person and guides you how to grow your business.

Richard encourages you and guides you through modules and group webinars. Mixing with our likeminded individuals who are happy to share their wins and losses is a great help. Richard makes you aware of the attention to detail! Having the support makes the difference as Richard is the most Approachable person.

I have managed to produce a salon manual and encourage my team to lead more. Coaching yourself and your team is the way forward.

One of my wins is increasing the teams income per client, setting goals and regular one to ones.

I could go on...!

Marina Hodgins, Fringe Benefits & La Bella Beauty, United Kingdom

Chapter 3 DELIVER

Deliver

One of the biggest problems salon owners face, is that they opened their salons because they were good at what they did. Someone may have set the seed that they should open their own salon because they will make lots of money and have lots of freedom. That seed was set and you started thinking because clients love you and you found it easy to build a clientele, it seems like the best thing to do.

Don't get me wrong it's great that clients love you, and you're good at what you do, and your desire to open a salon and service more clients is great. But the reality is, you're so busy looking after clients that you don't have the time to build a business, and your clients are so demanding that they will not give other staff the opportunity to look after them. So the business becomes all about you. Your business is you, and if you're not there the takings will drop, things will go wrong and the clients will not want anyone else to look after them and they are happy to wait until you get back in to work.

One thing is for certain you'll never be able to grow your salon into a Lifestyle Salon on your own, taking your salon from good to great, you will need help from others, you'll need a team. There is only so much time you have in your day and if you're fully booked working the floor, eventually you will burn out or lose your passion. This happens to a lot of salon owners that try to stay small. Time is the only commodity you sell as a salon owner and you have only so much time to give. Besides, the day you bought your salon, you became a business owner and that means your business is bigger than you.

So basically you need to sell more time, to free you up, to give you freedom to help drive the business forward, otherwise if no one is driving new clients into the salon or driving the business full stop, the business will start to decline.

To sell more time you need more staff and with that will come a few issues, as many of you may know already, if you have been in business for a while.

Because as your salon grows, your salon will have bigger problems and things will undoubtably go wrong. Things will undoubtably mess up and you will start to struggle to control everything on your own.

You will need good staff for your salon to thrive and grow.

Staff, the dreaded bane of any salon owner, we can't live with them, but we can't live without them!

To overcome the issues I was encountering as a boss, I created a system in my salon that turned all my problems and issues with my staff into a thing of the past.

You see I wasn't like other salon owners, I didn't have staff issues, my staff stayed around and worked for me for a long time, they hit targets, they turned up early to work, they worked late, they even told me off if I made a mistake. They celebrated when the salon hit its weekly targets, and felt deflated when we didn't. They cared for the clients, for me and for the salon. So why were my staff so different to other salon owners?

Well, if you remember my story at the beginning it wasn't always this way.

I decided to do something about it, and that changed my salon life forever.

So how do you fix the salon owners biggest bane of their life? The staff!

It's one of the biggest moans I hear from salon owners, it's always about their staff.

They moan they can't find staff.

No one applies for the job when it's advertised.

They moan about the staff they've got, that they're useless and rubbish and they have an attitude problem.

The say they don't do as they're told and they don't listen.

They're not happy with their staffs rebooks, they're too low, their retail is poor, they never hit targets.

The list of moans is endless!

The main issue I see with salon owners that moan about not finding staff, that the staff don't do as they are told and seem passionless and demotivated is that the boss just needs a few more skills to learn. They just don't know how to write a good ad, train their team to sell more, and to get better rebooks or to create a team culture.

So the blame gets put on the staff, but it's not the staffs fault, staff don't know any better.

The buck has to stop with you the owner.

To make your salon work, and to grow and without you being the busy fool, you need to systemise your salon. 'McDonaldise' your salon! To make every client visit remarkable and perfect if you are there or not, and to be able to train your team to deliver on this promise regardless of skill or attitude.

Imagine if you could systemise your salon and you knew that if the staff followed the system you could guarantee the amount of clients that would rebook, you would know the amount of retail that would be sold each day, and how many clients would stay loyal to your salon. Well, that's just what I did in my salon, I wanted to take the human error out of the equation and you can do that too.

Which means you can get any employee to follow a proven system.

I know what you're thinking; your staff don't do what they're told now. But I will teach you how to educate them, so it works, so they fall in love with systems.

If McDonalds can get a 15 year old to follow a basic system all around the world, a 15 year old that cannot even make their beds in the morning, then surely you can get your staff to sweep the floor, to clean up, to make coffee, to rebook, to sell retail with perfection time and time again.

You need to know how to break this down into an easy step by step procedure, so it's easy for them to understand.

Everything in your salon can be broken down into a basic system. So that everybody knows what needs to get done, by whom and by when it needs to be done.

This is a lot simpler than you think.

Almost every salon owner that comes to me as a coaching client wants to sell more retail, get more rebooks and more client retention. The 3 Rs.

They usually blame the staff and say that their staff aren't passionate, or motivated.

They just observe them and think that they're demotivated.

Your staff will never, ever be as passionate as you.

They shouldn't be as passionate as you. It's dangerous if they're as passionate as you.

If they're as passionate as you and as motivated as you they're going to leave you and open their own salon, we don't want them that passionate and that motivated do we?

You see you have a right to be passionate and motivated because it's your salon, you're going to take all the spoils, you're growing the business, it's all about your dream.

What you want to do is not rely on passion, but rely on a system and systemise their working day to make sure that when a client comes in, that they get treated exactly the same as if it were by you.

Most salon owners that I speak to and I'm sure you are the same, believe that if they could 10 times themselves, the salon would be pumping and they'd make lots of money.

What I want you to do is systemise your business, so it's like having 10 of you in the salon.

Imagine if you could control how much retail you sold, or how many clients rebooked, with a proven system you can do that, it would mean if you employed a new staff member you would know that they'd hit a certain amount of rebooks and retail right away, and the system is never going to leave you.

Systems don't have off days.

Systems don't have sick days.

Now we all know that we all have bad days, even me, even you.

What needs to happen is, you will want to make sure no matter how you feel, how your staff feel that when a client walks through your door they get treated exactly the same, every day of the week.

Imagine if a client comes in to your salon and you can map out a client journey, touch points where a staff member and client interact. What if you could train your staff on every touch point to up sell services and retail, to rebook and wow the client, that would give you the power to know that the clients would be wowed and you'd know before that client even walked through the door they were going to rebook, were going to buy retail and they would never leave your salon and stay loyal to you.

That's the power of systemising your business with a remarkable service and a client journey.

But don't you have enough to do already? Is this going to take up all of your time?

Nope, my motto is simple, "Do it once and do it right". You're working hard already, let's work smart and get some help.

We want your team, not just you, to hit your salon goals, but there's certain things they need to work out before they can do that.

Your salon needs systems, and systems control the sales.

You don't need a salon full of super stars, you just need super star systems.

Now you know the power of systems the next time you look to employ a staff member, stop looking for the holy grail. You see most salon owners want a staff member to come with a full clientele, who is great at retail, who is fantastic at rebooks. That's not what you should be looking for. That's dangerous and they're hard to find. Your job is to find that rough diamond. Someone who has the perfect attitude, and teach them the systems.

Remember business is people and people buy from people they like.

Tip: You need to employ someone who can smile 8 hours a day, who loves pleasing people and then you introduce them to your systems. You know clients will love them so they'll get booked out pretty quickly. I've never met a staff member that clients love that is not fully booked.

You'll know your systems work and will deliver your numbers so you teach them the systems.

Let the systems do all the hard lifting.

Let's dive in and do this together!

Remarkable Service

One of the key strategies to getting your salon to earn you more while you actually work less is the remarkable service that you offer. You'll be able to grow your salon and increase your income without adding any more hours to your day. This is about making your salon the destination not you.

Getting your salon standards perfected and systemised is like multiplying you by 10 times, and not making you the busiest person in the salon. Which in turn will free up your time to drive the salon that you've always dreamed of!

With clients nowadays looking for more loyalty and they're looking for salons that they can belong to, to be part of a community, and what comes with community is predictability. They need to feel that when they visit your salon they get the same result, time and time again. Be it on your quietest days or on your busiest days, you have to deliver an absolutely remarkable service.

Let's take a look at the masters of systemisation, McDonalds. They are the biggest, highest earning restaurant in the world, they're not the best of course but people go there because they know what to expect, it's predictable, when you walk through the door you know what to expect, that's comforting. If you feel that you can't even get your staff to make a decent coffee time and time again, or your staff to do as they are told, then you need to systemise your salon now.

If you don't systemise your salon you will be constantly moaning and nagging your staff for the rest of your salon life.

- You need to make your salon the destination and not you.
- You need to make your staff perform to their best ability

on your busiest day and on your quietest day, whether you're there or whether you're not there.

- You need to guarantee to the client that your salon will run impeccably to a high standard regardless of what time of day they arrive and regardless of whether you're there or not.

If you cannot replicate yourself and get your staff to be able to do a remarkable service then your clients will not try your staff they'll just demand that you look after them taking up more of your time. You will eventually lose your passion or burn out, I have seen this many times before, and your staff will get very bored and may even think about leaving you.

Getting your staff on board with this and everyone on the same page is easier than you think. They'll get to know your core story and your dream and they get to live it too. So when clients come into the salon the culture is in everything your salon does and you're actually walking the walk, and talking the talk.

I believe you will want to take the error away from human hands so that when things go wrong in the salon you don't have to reprimand the staff, you get to reprimand the system. Which is always your fault by the way, which means you get to fix the system and the problem!

Believe it or not your staff will be happier with systems in place because everybody will know where they stand. It won't be down to your mood or how you feel on the day or you reacting to the pressure of not affording to pay bills this month.

What tends to happen in many salons is that the salon owner is too friendly with the staff and cannot reprimand them, or swings the opposite way and tells everyone off, all the time, they'll have a laugh in the backroom with their staff members and they'll let some things go, they might see a client not being asked to rebook and don't say anything, they'll let it go this time, they'll see a consultation not being done properly and they'll let it go again and they'll see a bit of hair on the floor and they'll let it go also, and a staff member will be 5 minutes late for work and they'll let it go, and then suddenly the salon owner snaps and let's rip. What usually happens then is there's a big pow wow in the backroom between you and half a dozen staff members and then every staff member in the backroom talks about you saying, "Ooh what's the matter with you, you've gone a bit moody".

You will feel they have no respect for you, and they think you must be having a bad day.

This is one of the common reasons that staff leave, they just don't know where they stand with you.

Having systems in place keeps you accountable as well as your staff.

The clients need to know that no matter what happens they are guaranteed a remarkable service.

We know in the real world it's hard, a staff member comes to work and they may have fallen out with their partner, another might have their dog sick, or their mum or dad might be sick, they might just be having a bad day, or they just don't feel the love today.

But clients don't need to know this, they shouldn't need to know this. I was always told, "Leave all your rubbish at the door", it's easier for everyone.

You see just because their mind is elsewhere and not on the job, we don't want them to forget to give the client a great service, make them coffee, give the client love, or even give them too much love, that's just as bad.

One of my staff had a terrible habit, and when she reads this she will know it's about her.

She used to roll her eyes at clients, behind their backs, not nasty, just if a clients asked her for the impossible, it was a bad habit. I used to tell her that there are mirrors everywhere and clients see everything. Because they do! So always be aware, everything you do, good or bad is being seen by someone in the salon.

If you imagine that on one of your busy days a client comes in to complain or something goes wrong and you're running around like a headless chicken, making it up on the fly and your staff are running around like headless chickens too. Your clients will see this and will feel uncomfortable.

Your staff will feel your uncomfortableness and so will the clients. You cannot keep making it up as you go. Winging it! You will also look really unprofessional.

Professional salons get two things right:

1.   If you're more professional you'll get more 5 star reviews as your clients will want to tell the world about your salon.
2.   You'll get more money, you can charge more and you will get more referrals because clients will refer people to you if they know you give a professional service time and time again. If you want to charge more in your salon then you need to act more professionally.

You need to be the expert.

You need to get your salon to run without you, without your input.

Imagine a client comes into your salon today, and has a complaint, this is how most salons deal with a complaint:

It all starts with a person walking in the salon and they head towards the reception area, the salon goes a little quiet because people recognise this person as only just having been to the salon. You, the owner notice her too.

They usually speak to maybe the receptionist or an apprentice, because they're usually the ones who are free. The client explains that they're not happy with maybe the haircut, the waxing or whatever service they've had. The staff member calls over the person who did the service and that person leaves their client that they are attending to and go and see what the problem is, they've got their back up already, a little embarrassed they head to the reception area and go on the defensive, just saying no, no, no, you asked for this, and there's a bit of a raucous at the front desk.

Then the client asks to speak to the manager, or you eventually come over to the reception, to help the situation.

Now picture this, there's now four people at the reception desk having a heavy discussion, the rest of the clients in the salon are seeing what's going on and at this stage it's looking like there's a massive complaint going on, bigger than it actually is, and what are you going to do that every other staff member could not do?

Are you going to argue with this client? Or are you going to deal with it?

Most owners deal with it regardless of what the complaint is. But what just happened?

You've been taken off your service, it could be a haircut or a colour or a massage and you've left a client to come and deal with a complaint. The other staff member left a client to come and deal with a complaint and you've got another 2 people hanging around the reception desk. The client with the complaint is now feeling like you're ganging up on her and she's got her back up so she's responding in a defensive way.

You've got your back up because she's got her back up and nothing gets resolved and I assure you that you've lost that client.

And every other client in the salon is now scared to complain to you because of the scene it causes.

That's what generally happens in most salons today.

Resolve a complaint in the customer's favour and they will do business with you again 70% of the time.

What I did in my salon was I built a system.

Here's my system:

My Complaint System

I had a book and I called it, 'Client Complaint Book'.

I held a team meeting and told my staff how I wanted a client complaint dealt with. We role played every situation out, so they knew that they could handle the toughest complaint. I then documented the step by step process and included it into my salon policy and procedures manual.

I gave my staff the authority to deal with any complaint on their own, I gave every single staff member including the apprentice the authority to give money back to a client if they weren't happy regardless of whose fault it was.

This is how we dealt with a general complaint when in my salon:

If a client came in to complain, they would speak to a staff member and say they're not happy, my staff would say, we've got a 100% guarantee or it's free, if you're not 100% happy for any reason it's free, and we will fix it too, if you want us to.

They would give the client their money back there and then, get her to fill out the complaint in the 'Client Complaint Book', making notes of what was wrong, and why the client didn't like it.

Then the client would sign the page and they would give her the money back.

At the end of the day I would check the book to see if we had had any complaints. If there were this is what I would do next. I would phone the client and I would explain that I'm really sorry there was an issue, and ask them to please come back in because we would love a chance to rectify it, and 9 out of 10 times if we dealt with a client complaint like that we would win over the client and now we would have a client for life.

Now how simple is that!

One simple system that transformed the salon and made us look very professional, and that means I can carry on with my clients or I don't get a phone call on my day off to say someone's come in with a complaint. My staff had the authority to deal with it there and then.

Getting your staff to handle some of the work load makes it so much easier for you to concentrate on more important matters and drive your salon business.

If you can get all your staff to give a great service that's the same as multiplying yourself by 10 times. If only you could, but we cannot multiply ourselves 10 times but this is the next best thing.

Let it be your systems wowing the clients not the staff.

Many years ago my coach taught me that the day of the super star staff member is over, clients want experience first and foremost.

A great hairdresser with poor customer service skills would not grow their salon faster or make as much money as an average skilled hairdresser with exceptional customer service skills.

I am living proof of this.

To confirm this you only need to check out what most people are buying as Christmas presents today , most people buy experiences. Look how fast Red Letter Day grew their business. It's all about the experience.

We are going through an era where people are happy to pay good money to get a great experience.

Customer service is dead, long live the experience.

And that's never been truer than it is today.

Clients come to you for the experience. Think about why a client would choose your salon that charges $100 for a haircut as opposed to a salon down the road that charges $25 for the same job.

Clients don't know the difference between the haircuts. So they judge you on how they feel when they are in the salon and the feeling when they leave, they do want nice coffee, they do want nice magazines, some do want nice music, some do want iPads to search the internet and some do want free wifi.

Clients want the experience they don't want to be rushed.

The clients that are looking for a cheaper alternative will go somewhere else that's fast and they don't care about the experience at all. But if you want to set your salon up where clients are paying a bit more money then you've got to put an experience in your salon and that means that you've got to be able to replicate that experience over and over again, with you there or with you not there, and the only way to do that is to build a remarkable service system.

Clients need predictability.

We live in a busy world and clients need to know they can organise their busy schedule around your salon. And know that it's predictable.

They're busy with their children, they're busy with their jobs and they need to know that when they come into your salon and whoever looks after them, they will deliver the same result in the same amount of time, every time. If they come to you and you do a half heads of foils and a cut and blow dry in 3 hours they expect it to take 3 hours with every staff member, every visit, all of the time.

They don't want to come once and it's 2 hours and next time they come it's 3 hours. That's not what they're after here.

Do not take advantage of them.

If you can get this system right in your salon, clients will fall in love with the experience you deliver and they'll be less likely to follow a staff member if that staff member leaves you.

Staff love systems too, they might offer a little friction when you start implementing it, but staff love the fact that the salon is run fairly, with all staff members, every time, it makes the staff so much happier.

Happy staff take 10 times less sick days per year!

It's a joy to work in a salon that's systemised. It creates a great team and a great salon culture.

I want to share with you how important being consistent is in the real world.

A coffee shop opened two doors down the road from my salon.

It advertised the best chicken salad in the world. I don't normally eat at lunch times but Thursday was my late night and felt that I needed some food to keep my strength up.

I sent my apprentice down the road to ask for the 'best chicken salad in the world' I was not disappointed, it was immense. That week I told all of my clients how great my lunch was. I recommended so many people to go to that coffee shop and try their 'best salad in the world'.

I couldn't wait until next Thursday, it really was the best chicken salad in the world. Next week came around and I took my break a little early to get my chicken salad and I could not believe it OMG it was beautiful, they'd surpassed themselves, it was fantastic, it was the best chicken salad in the universe. How could they make it any better I thought? Well, I told everybody again for a whole week about how good it was. I think I must have sent in over 100 clients to try it out. I was singing their praises all over town.

I couldn't wait until the following Thursday. What was it going to be like, the anticipation.

Well, next Thursday couldn't come around fast enough, but it did, I sent my apprentice to get me my favourite chicken salad, I couldn't wait, I'd booked an extra 15 minutes so I could eat it without having to rush it.

Well, you would never guess what happened next?

The apprentice returned and the salad looked amazing, I started eating it and I was quite disappointed. Not because it was bad it wasn't it was still exceptional. They'd delivered the best chicken salad in the world just like the first one I raved about all week.

But I now felt cheated. I felt cheated because I know that they can do better and now I felt like I've got something substandard.

They don't have to deliver a bad chicken salad, to be honest they were all exceptional but I just felt cheated somehow.

You see it's not about offering bad service, you've just got to deliver the same service every single time. This is what's going to lift your business higher than ever before, make you charge more, make your clients stay longer and make your staff stay longer, it's going to make you more money and free up more of your time.

A typical salon owner only hears from 4% of dissatisfied clients.

That means that 96% of clients that aren't going to complain, that are not happy, will just walk away from your salon and you will not even know why.

That should make you love your clients complaining because that gives you the opportunity to fix the problem before they leave.

On average 86% of clients quit doing business with a salon because of a bad customer experience.

This stuff matters.

Imagine you are going to a restaurant with your partner and you both order the same meal, and out comes the same two meals, let's say you ordered steak, mushrooms and fries. Two basic meals. One of those meals comes out and it's got the biggest, juiciest steak and a big pile of hot fries and loads of buttered mushrooms swimming in a beautiful garlic sauce.

The next meal comes out with a small piece of steak and a few fries on the side and the same buttery mushrooms only not as many as on the other plate. Now looking at these two plates, one of you will feel super elated, but the other is going to feel really cheated, but what I can guarantee is that you will not go back to that restaurant again, because of little inconsistencies in the kitchen you now feel awkward, and that's how your clients feel in your salon.

If one of your team members is spoiling their clients, maybe it's a quiet day and they are giving them an extra long massage or spending longer on a service than usual, all of the other clients in the salon are noticing what's going on, and they are either thinking, that's a trainee doing that because they're taking too long or why is she getting all that love and I'm getting none?

You see both clients are feeling uncomfortable, the client who's getting spoilt and the client who's not being spoilt are both thinking different things.

You definitely don't want that in your salon, you will want to make sure that every client that comes into your salon gets the best service by every team member, all of the time.

Because bad news travels twice as fast as good news!

You'll get more clients talking about your salon saying not to go to that salon, than recommending to go to you.

I know you have a dream and your salon is part of that dream, remember your dream, your goal at all times.

That dream will consist of how you want your salon to look, how you want your clients treated and how you want your staff to behave.

You start that dream now, by setting a minimum standard in your salon.

Your salon needs to set some sort of standards. A minimum standard that you expect and a minimum that a client expects when they walk through the door.

Setting your salon standards is paramount to getting your salon to be busy in todays world.

This way all the staff will know what's expected of them to achieve the minimum standard. They will all be on the same page as you (which results in less nagging).

This is how you offload some of the heavy lifting needed to grow your salon, get your team to help you achieve your dream.

You build these systems with your team at team meetings.

Call a team meeting this week and start to build your minimum standards, your salons policies and procedures.

Every salon that I have worked at has had issues with who's responsible for what job.

An old fashioned staff member will say it's the apprentices role to do all the dirty and mundane jobs, because they had to do it when they were training. But the modern salon owner will understand it's everyones job to keep the salon up to scratch. They should all be helping you make your dream come true.

The mundane jobs like folding the towels, cleaning the tools, cleaning the windows, making the clients coffee, answering the phone, etc, we all know no-one wants to do them and are happy to pass them on to apprentices or trainees's, but it's everyones job and it's your role to get these done to perfection with every staff member, without nagging.

And I don't know any better way to make sure all these jobs are done, than building a system to make sure it's all done to perfection.

If you systemise this really well it's everyones job not just one persons and everyone builds the system together, so they own the system and want to make sure it never gets broken, and the salon looks impeccable at all times.

You then document it, and you use this as a training schedule.

You see once you systemise your business, every single item that is systemised becomes your training manual for new staff members. As a new staff member starts with you, you can onboard them with your system manuals and life just becomes so much easier.

You can print out all of your manuals and keep them handy, give the new staff member the system and you say, "Hey this is the system of how we clean or fold towels, or mix up colour, this is how we do it here, take this home and learn it, this is the way we like it done in our salon".

You can have a system for cleaning, answering the phone, rebooking, retail, client complaints, making coffee, you name it, it can be done with almost anything in your salon.

This will McDonaldise your salon business so much that your salon will be running almost to perfection with or without you being there.

I used this strategy in my salon for many years and got my team to train the new staff members so that I didn't have to be the one to do it.

It's very easy when your staff help you build the systems as opposed to you doing all the work. If you systemise your business it will become a cash cow. One day if you ever want to sell it will be worth twice as much if your salon is systemised than if it's not.

I want to finish showing you how important this really is.

I had a client that I looked after for 3 years, I loved doing this clients hair, she came every 3 weeks to have her colour touched up and we always had a laugh together. You know the sort of client I mean. When you see them booked in, you just know that you're going to have a good day.

Then one day she just stopped coming. I didn't know why she stopped coming, she just stopped. I missed her, the same as you probably miss some of your good clients when you lose them. But six months later I bumped into her in my town centre and I called her name and I said, "Hey it's been eating away at me for a while, I'd love to know what happened, did I do something wrong?" and she said "I'm really sorry Richard I loved the haircut you gave me, I loved the colour too but your apprentice gave me a coffee one day and it had a lipstick stain on the cup", and then she said "I just couldn't come back, I thought to myself, if their coffee cup was dirty, their combs could be dirty, their scissors could be dirty, their chairs could be dirty, their towels could be dirty, I just couldn't bring myself to come back, I'm sorry", I said, "It's ok I get that".

That was the day I realised that I had to systemise my business. Being good at what I did was not good enough anymore. Losing one of my best clients over something so simple really got to me.

It could be happening in your salon right now as we speak. Clients will walk away from your business because of an indifference of time, an indifference of service and nothing to do with the work that they're paying for. They just feel that you are no longer good value for money or you're taking them for granted.

This is how the average salon loses its clients:

1% Die
3% Move out of the area
5% Follow a friends advice to go to another salon
9% Find a salon that they feel offers a better service
14% Move salons because they are actually dissatisfied with the results you give them.
68% Leave because of indifference, they don't feel valued or special anymore. They don't feel the love.

This is a massive loss to any salon and should be your number one priority.

Systemising your business sets you apart from any other salon in town.

It's what will get your business to the wow factor and more.

Almost 9 out of 10 clients say they would pay more to ensure a superior customer experience.

Competing on price isn't the most effective way to build your business. Great service, delivered time and time again is.

Will it be simple? Yes

Will it be easy? No

But the rewards will far outweigh the costs.

Now go book that team meeting!

CASE STUDY

Loving the modules, I love actually going back and tweeking as I learn more from each module it gives me more of an awareness.

Eg- Vip policy and branding and values etc

I love the one on one calls - it makes a huge impact to get a kick in the bum- everyone can keep themselves accountable for certain periods of time but nice to get pointed in the right direction as I steer off course sometimes.

A win for me would be- I was literally like the titanic sinking down when I let go of my second salon which put me in a lot of debt, when I first talked to rich, but with a lot of hard work I still have a salon and it's slowly growing. I even had all

My staff leave at one stage and I was looking after 60 clients a week on my own with no help, but loved the encouragement I received from Richard, Nicole and the group and kept me sane :)

I know have an amazing team, and my aim will be to expand the salon when all debt is paid off and I have some $ behind me

I love how Richard is honest and blunt and know where you stand

I liked that the modules are easy to understand and step by step and always doing a video a week and repetition.

Love all of the marketing ones lately the best! To attract new client but also love the processes to keep clients in the door

Dana, Beautify Hair Design, Queensland, Australia

Client Satisfaction Mastery

Most salon owners that I coach seem to have the same problem, they seem to have a problem with their client retention being poor, retail sales not being good enough and low rebooks. They complain that the staff are not passionate, but what they really mean is they are not rebooking or selling retail. And a lot of salon owners find it really hard to get their staff to hit set targets because they don't want to upset them. If you master the client satisfaction mastery, if you get this right your retail, your rebooks and your client retention will go through the roof naturally.

You see clients like predictability and they like to feel comfortable and most clients do like to buy, they just don't like being sold to.

Clients who visit your salon are now judging you on experiences that they get in their world. This means if they've gone and bought a BMW from a BMW dealer and received a remarkable service they're going to judge your salon by that service.

If they went out for a meal the night before and that restaurant was spectacular and the service was impeccable and they had a beautiful time then they'll expect and judge your salon on the service they got from that restaurant. That's the world we're living in. That's the world your clients are living in.

The old way used to be, as a long as you were better than the salon down the road, you just needed to offer better service, colour, waxing, music coffee, teas or biscuits, but the new way clients are judging you on experiences they get in their world, and if you want to charge more for what you do you need to lift your game because if you want clients that are used to paying good money that means they're used to getting an impeccable service, a remarkable service elsewhere in their world.

You need to lift your game!

If you are anything like me, when I go out to a restaurant and the food is beautiful, the service is impeccable and attentive, and they treated me like a king and every element of that nights experience in the restaurant was spectacular. When the bill arrives I just don't query it, I think it's good value for money. I've had a really good time, they've looked after me really well, the food was impeccable and I pay the bill (to be honest I don't even look at it).

But if the waitress wasn't so kind, if she didn't get my wine when I wanted one, if they made me wait for my main course for ages, if my steak was undercooked, if my dessert had taken too long to come out, if my coffee was cold then I start picking at the bill because I'm dissatisfied, and sometimes it's nothing to do with the food it's to do with the service.

Your clients are no different.

If you want your clients to pay good money to come to your salon, every element of the client journey needs to be impeccable, and that means working out a client journey in your salon that you can work on and tweak and make sure at every single stage of the journey that your client travels through with any member of staff is second to none.

Your clients need to be treated with an impeccable amount of tenderness and love with you being there or not.

With client loyalty at an all time low it's never been more important to get this right.

We know that the average salon is losing 24% of their regular clients every year.

Work on this strategy and make them numbers work in your favour.

Make your clients stay more loyal.

We also know that new client retention is shocking, the average salon is losing around 75% of its first time clients.

Yep, re-read that statement, it's shocking isn't it!

They say when a new client walks through your door you have only got 20 seconds to win them over, that's it, only a short 20 seconds.

Just shouting to that new client, "Come over Tracey, take a seat here", doesn't work anymore.

Neither is grunting at them to take a seat and going off to finish a client.

So you have 20 seconds to make this client feel at home and wanting to be a client of yours, that's all you've got.

If you worked on greeting this client better in those first 20 seconds you can easily save yourself at least 25% loss to your business. That's massive, that's 25% increase to your salons takings with NO marketing, it's worth working on don't you think?

So you need to get all of your staff on the same page so they can all treat the clients with the same love and care, every single day.

You will need to do a little bit of work for them, to break the client journey down into smaller bites, so it's easy for them to learn, practice and understand that every step of the journey has an important role in winning over the clients. This also makes it easy for you to track every step, and see your staffs weak points.

This way all the staff know where they stand and what their weak points are, so they can master the client journey and get fully booked with high paying clients.

Setting Salon Standards

You will need to set some salon standards in your salon. It doesn't have to be complicated, or difficult. Salon standards are just that. Standards that you think are acceptable as a minimum that your staff can achieve.

You can call them KPIs, salon standards or policies and procedures, it's just the minimum that you expect your service and salon to be run by.

This way you get to discipline the failure of the salon standard and not the person. It makes it so much easier for you to lead your team and still be a close friend and so much easier for the staff member because they know what they have to do to please you and keep the salon growing.

Your job is to let them all know where this line is that you're going to call your salon standard.

A salon standard isn't just KPI's or numbers that the staff have to hit, it's also how you want your clients to be treated and how you want the salon atmosphere and culture to be.

So what is your salon standard?
What numbers are important to you?
How do you want your clients treated?
These will be what matters to you.

My salon standard KPI's were quite low and I know many people would say too low. But hey I was happy with them.

I'll share them later on in this chapter.

How good would it be if you could guarantee your service 100%?

We are all human and we all make mistakes but what if you can take away the human error from your salon results, what if you could systemise the whole thing so that as long as the staff followed a pattern, a system, you could guarantee the results. Wouldn't that be just amazing? Your salon performing as you want without your salon suffering from a certain staff members attitude, because they're having a bad day or anything else that's going wrong in the salon.

If you can get your staff on their best and worst day to replicate a certain system of how that client gets treated, wouldn't that be a good thing.

Most salon owners I speak to are looking for that super star to walk in to their salon and make them lots of money, they want the best rebooks, with most clients, selling the most retail and smashing targets. But if you've ever had a salon long enough and you've had some superstars working for you, superstars you love them when they arrive, they bring clients with them, they are high earners they're hitting targets, they're selling retail their rebooks are great, you love them.

But they come with a lot of attitude, a bit of a chip on their shoulders, but you tend to put up with it because they are making you good money.

I couldn't imagine working in a salon with five of them, and the quick thought is you'll be making lots of money, it'll be great.

But it would be a horrible place to work, wouldn't it?

If you've been in business long enough you're going to know one thing and if you don't know this yet, it may be brewing as we speak.

Superstars don't stay around for long, they have other agendas.

They came to you with lots of clients because they took them from their old salon and when they leave your salon they're going to take a bunch of your clients too.

You're going to feel the drop hugely. They'll leave with your clients.

They may even open a salon down the road, they may even take some of your staff members with them.

So if you get this salon standard system right, you don't need a salon full of superstars to make lots of money.

You're much better off with a salon full of average performing workers that are following a superstar system and that way the system always stays with the salon, your salon. Not only that but the average performing staff member loves working for you because it's the only place they can hit their commissions, the only place their rebooks are up, the only place their retail is through the roof, and they belong to something bigger than themselves.

Taking time out of your busy day and working through this client journey is going to save you an awful lot of time in the long run.

It's going to change the way you work in your salon forever.

Most people are pleasers and will always aim to please you. Most people only do enough to please though, enough to pass, enough to get by and stay out of trouble.

So your role in setting up a salon standard is to make it achievable to all. A standard that the clients love, and a standard that your staff can achieve.

Draw your salon standard line.

What do your staff have to do to stay above that line?

Then most staff will lift their game to stay just above the line, that's fine, you get the odd employee that will smash it, but most will stay just above.

This will give you certain numbers to work towards.

It also lets the staff know what is expected of them. Everyone knows the rules and it's a fair playing game.

This then relieves you of the pressure of disciplining your staff.

You see most owners find it really hard to discipline their staff, because we're social butterflies we like to hang around with our friends, we spend time together, you know you go out drinking with them, you socialise with them and then something goes wrong in the salon and you either have to let it go or you have to discipline them. It's awkward for you and for them. That's only because they don't know where they stand (no line is drawn) and you feel you're telling your friend off and they may take it the wrong way.

This way if you set your salon standards right they know it's their fault already, they know they've dropped below the line of the salon standards and I assure you they will know a quick chat is coming, they are expecting it.

The last thing you want to be is a nagger!

You don't want to be nagging them all the time because their rebooks are low, their retail is low, they'll just think you're interested in money.

They will think you are greedy.

They'll just think they can never please you.

This way you set the system up with what needs to get done, you teach them the system and if the system fails you just pick them up on it with a quick follow up chat, really simple.

This is what I did, it's easy:

"Hey Beth can I have a quick word with you in the back room. You know our consultations are done a certain way?" Beth replies, "Yes", and then I continue with, "Well I noticed your rebooks are dropping so I watched you today and I realised that you're not doing the consultation correctly you're missing this stage out. In our next team meeting let's do some role playing to make sure we get that done", and Beth will reply with, "Yes".

Of course she knows that she's not done it she's just got lazy or she's got something else on her mind. But this way she knows that you're following through on a standard that she's agreed to.

This is going to make your life really easy in the long run because when the staff know that you're following through, when the staff know that you'll discipline the system not them, it's not personal, they won't take it personally, you get to be their friend, they get to know they need to lift their game and it's nice and simple.

When I employed a new staff member I told them this on the first day they worked for me, "These are the minimum standards I expect in my salon, I'm going to give you the tools and show you how to do this, but if you fall below the line, I'm going to have to pick you up on it because the salon has a certain standard to live up to, that our clients have come to expect from us, and if you personally fall below it I'm going to show you exactly where you're falling below and how to lift your game". They now know that you're very serious about this and will follow through, and of course you are going to discipline the system, not them.

It's time to set your salon standards, but first let's take a look at this example of a great customer service

SUPPORT THE FOUNDATIONS WITH SYSTEMS

Delighting The Customer

You go to book your car in for a service. On the other end of the phone is a polite and well mannered service manager who asks you a series of questions to ensure that the booking goes smoothly.

"Can I have your name please?"

"Your contact number?"

"What day and time are you looking to book the car in for a service?"

"Your car model and registration number?"

"How many kilometres has the car done?"

"Have you experienced any problems with the car?"

"Would you like to use one of our courtesy cars for only $10, or we can arrange a complimentary shuttle bus to take you to the nearest train or bus station?"

At the end of the conversation, you take up the offer of a courtesy car, and you feel assured that your car will be in safe hands as it is being serviced. The day before the car is due for its service you receive a text message on your mobile phone:

"Miss Jones, just a reminder that your car is booked in for tomorrow at 7:30am, and that your courtesy car will be here waiting for you. If you have any questions please contact Stan on 0000 1111."

You take your car in for the service. The service office is immaculately clean and resembles a hotel lobby. The smell of freshly brewed coffee is in the air, and you ask yourself, "How come I cannot smell any car fumes?" The service manager greets you, is well dressed in a neatly pressed shirt and tie, with a name badge. You give him the keys, and he asks you, "Do you mind if I go through our 12 Point Service Guarantee?" He then places the form in front of you, and points his pen next to each of the guarantees as he explains each one to you.

You then drive off in the courtesy car. The car is the latest model, and it drives fantastically. As you are driving it, you say to yourself that this will be your next car. You are phoned later in the day by the service manager to tell you the car is ready for pick up. On your arrival, your car is waiting at the front of the office, and has been cleaned inside and out. Before you are about to pay, the service manager goes through all of the service points that were carried out. You do not even care about how much the service cost, because it was so good.

A couple of days later, Suzie from the customer care department of the dealership, gives you a courtesy call. She asks you a few non-intrusive questions about your thoughts on the service, the performance of the car, or any questions that you may have about the whole experience. The car is working perfectly, and you are totally satisfied by the experience, and you love the fact that the dealership wanted to know your thoughts.

Here is an example of a perfect link between what the dealership had in mind as they were creating the vision, mission, values, and unique selling proposition for their business, and what the customer wants from any engagement. Can you see how the dealership has built a system?

1. When you contacted the dealership the service had a script for taking bookings.
2. The dealership also had a reservation system to offer you a courtesy car or complimentary shuttle bus. The dealership had worked out the greatest issue when customers booked their car in for service, was how were people going to get from the dealership to their next destination.

3.   A day before the service, a reminder text was sent to you. The dealership understood that in these hectic times we sometimes forget different appointments that we've made.

4.   On your arrival the service staff had uniforms and name badges so that you could identify them with ease. Before they serviced your car, they go through another script - the 12 Point Service Guarantee. From all the current affair shows that expose dodgy car services, consumers have a general fear of being cheated on what they have paid for. The 12 Point Service Guarantee reduces the fear in the purchase, in highlighting that the dealership will deliver on their promise.

5.   The courtesy car that is provided is also a system. It is a marketing system that is designed to get you hooked on the latest model of cars. Car manufacturers have done thousands of studies on the impact that driving a new car has on future purchases.

6.   Upon your arrival, your car is cleaned inside and out. In a time poor society we sometimes find it difficult to clean our cars, and the dealership again has saved you time and money.

7.   When you collect your car, the service manager goes through another script with you, explaining all the service points that were done to your car. This is again to reduce the fear in your mind, that you have received what you paid for.

8.   The follow-up phone call is to gain customer feedback on the service. The dealership records all of the information, and discusses it in team meetings. Any issues that are raised are quickly dealt with.

The systems that have been developed by the dealership have been well thought out. The systems have always focused on the customer first, prior to the needs of the business first. This is always a challenge for many businesses, as we try to make our life easier, instead of the customers, and in doing so, lose a lot of business because we have created barriers to make the purchase easier.

(extract taken from The Pillars of business Success, by Tony Gattari)

Setting up your salon standards

I want to share with you now my salon standards and how to set your salon standard in your salon.

My KPI'S or salon standards were:
Rebooks 65%
Retail 10%
Retention 80%
Booked out every week 80%
Wage Percentage 30%

As for the clients we had a strict client journey, as it was all about the client and giving them so much love.

Step 1 - Greeting - Every client was greeted by their first name on arrival and sat down with a consultation sheet and a drinks menu, within 10 seconds.
Step 2 - Consultation - Every client was given an in depth consultation every single time.
Step 3 - The wash - Every wash consisted of 2 minute shampoo, 3 minute shampoo, 5 minute condition and massage and all clients were offered a treatment which came with a 5 minute massage.
Step 4 - Show and tell - This is where we did the cut and colour work.
Step 5 - The reception, all clients were asked to rebook or buy retail.

Take a quick look at the image below. You will see 5 circles (Stages)on the page, this is a typical salon it has 5 steps that the client walks through as they travel through your salon.

NOTE - if you're a beauty salon, a nail salon or a spa you might only have 4 points, therefore I'd like you to miss #3 out.

Let's take a look at this system.

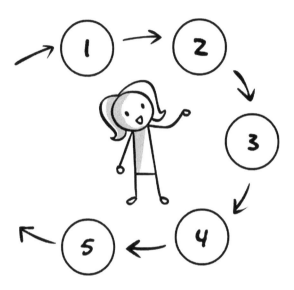

Step 1 is the greeting, nice and easy it's where you have those 20 seconds to get that new client looked after beautifully. What you need to do is greet every single person by their name. They've booked in the computer system so it's very simple you know that Mary's due at 12 o'clock and as 12 o'clock comes and a lady walks in the salon and you know it must be Mary, so say, " Hi Mary". But if someone walks in the salon and it's not Mary, just say, "Oops sorry we were expecting a Mary at 12 o'clock, do you have an appointment?". It's not the end of the world if you get their name wrong. Also if two clients are due in at the same time, just guess, it's a 50/50 after all. At least they will know that you are friendly.

Give them whatever consultation form you use to fill in, and give them a drinks menu (if you use one), and ask them which drink they'd like. Explain to them how far away you are from starting their service, and always keep them in the loop if you are running late. You would then give them their drink and let them know you'll be 5 minutes from now (or however long it's going to be). Pretty Simple.

Make them feel at home. It's a bit like you baking some cookies for me as I arrive at your house for a chat. You are heading upstairs to finish getting dressed and you say, " Help yourself to some cookies they are in the fridge", I would feel wrong going in the fridge so I'd just say, " I'm ok", but put those cookies on the table and say to me the same thing, "Help yourself to some cookies", I would definitely have one or two. Because I feel more comfortable, more at home. Your client needs to feel that comfort.

Step 2 This is where the magic happens, the consultation. You give the client the consultation form they've filled in, you've checked out what they need to get done, the stylist or therapist or whoever's going to deal with this client is going to come over and have a chat about what's going to happen through the client journey. You'll sit with them and ask them questions, what their problem is and how you can fix it, explain what the solution is.

We have a really great 6 point consultation that's guaranteed to lift your retail and your rebooks through the roof, our clients use this in our Lifestyle Salon Systems, that's our signature course.

Whatever it is, that you use to do your consultation, this is the time to do it. This is where the client will agree on price, they'll agree on what they are having done, they'll agree that you're ready to fix it for them, and will verbally agree the deal.

Step 3 This is the basin area, and this is our first opportunity to up sell them a treatment, to get your average bill up, but also it's a place where you can give them so much love. Most clients when asked say that this is the best part about visiting a salon, so make this memorable. This is a quiet area where you get to show a bit of love, and help them to clean out their worries for the day and get them ready for step 4.

Step 4. This is all about show and tell. If you've got your consultations done correctly then #4 is just about show and tell. It's about showing them what you said you would do for them at #2, it's telling them and educating them on what they need to do to make their hair, skin, nails look good when they're not in the salon. It's also the time where you set the seeds. You'll set a seed to rebook here, you'll set a seed to buy retail. This is where you actually get to shine and show off your work, it's what they came in for. During the service, you'll set all the seeds, you'll show them what needs to get done , you'll tell them how they can recreate this at home and how they can maintain this at home. To sum up, this is all about educating the client.

Step 5 The reception area. All the hard work should be done by now, everything should have been covered. At this stage it should simply be, "Did we manage to please you today Mary?" and that's it.

The client should know if they are rebooking already, they should know if they are buying retail. So you just rebook them in and wave them off.

So what do you need to do now to set up your systems?

Once you have this all set up in the salon, each stage will have an impact on your salons numbers.

If you play with words at stage 1 will it increase your new clients retention?

If you do an in depth consultation at stage 2 with an iPad will it increase your retail?

If you devise a new way to ask for treatments will you sell more?

If you educate the client at stage 4 and give the staff member an extra 5 minutes to teach the client how to get different results, will the client buy more retail?

If you honestly thank the clients at stage 5 will your rebooks go up?

Everything you do in this system from stages 1 - 5 will either lift your numbers or decrease your numbers and your role as the owner is to watch the system, tweak how you say things, tweak how you do things and increase the numbers with ease.

Here's an example:

You walk into a clothes shop and the first thing that the attendant says to you is, "Can I help you?" and you reply, "No I'm ok thank you", your brain hasn't even registered what they said, you know you needed help but you've just said no and now you can't do anything about it, but you're not ok and you'll spend the next 20 minutes looking around the shop for something to catch your eye. Why do we just automatically say? "No, I'm ok thank you".

You'll probably end up wandering out of the shop as well and maybe go into another one.

That attendant has just lost a sale.

How many sales is she losing the shop?

So let's say 100 people visit that shop every day and 60 leave without buying anything.

Now as the owner you should notice that 60 people are leaving without buying, and it's your role to tweak this number. To come up with a system to make more people buy.

What if you tried this?

What if you took the attendant and said, from now on I want to try something new, something that we are trialling out.

From now on when someone walks into this clothes shop I want you to say to them, "Hi my name is Beth if you can't find what you're looking for give me a yell, that's what I'm here for, on the left side of the shop we have all our new season stuff, and just behind me here, is all the discounted, end of season stuff, if you can't find your size, give me a yell as I know where all the sizes are, I'm here to help you today".

Now let's say 60 or 70 people buy and 30 people leave without buying anything, wouldn't you then change that to be your new system?

Wouldn't you then roll this out across every store that you owned. That's your way of doing it because that's what worked.

So if you systemise your business you can track the numbers then tweak your systems to increase the numbers.

Take this to your team and try something new, and see if the numbers increase.

Here's an example:

"Hey would you like to rebook?" That system gives you a 40% rebook rate,

"Can I book you in the diary Mary?" gives you a 65% rebook rate.

Which one are you going to go with? Of course the second one. Let's say you go back and you tweak that again and you play around with it for 6 weeks and the numbers go up again, that then becomes your new way in the salon.

So in your salon choose something that's working well or something that's not working well and change the way you do it and monitor it for 6 weeks and see if your numbers change.

Did they increase, or decrease?

If it's increased that's your new way. Roll it out, train your staff.

That is now your 'new salon standard', 'that's how you do it here' and that's how you grow your salon to get your salon to be remarkable.

To master the client journey is to set your salon apart from every salon in town.

Your job as the salon owner is to notice what the numbers are doing and drop or fix which system is faulting, have a quick word with your team, to let them know that you're following through, that you take this very seriously.

I guarantee you, this will change the way you manage your salon forever.

This will grow your salon faster than any other strategy.

This is what clients are searching for, so master this and you will be well on your way to having the Lifestyle you desire.

CASE STUDY

1.   I have only just started in January so I probably have a

huge amount to learn but in this first month I have learnt how to think about what the clients are looking for in presenting an ad.

2. Thinking outside of the box to be more creative
3. I have had one group meeting which I liked and the private page is great
4. I presented my fist ad and the engagement so far has been good

Diane Greven, Standing Ovations Hair & Beauty, VIC, Australia

Team Meeting Planner

Great businesses don't just happen, they become great businesses because of their employees. And a great salon is no exception. To make your salon great you will need a team of strong believers of your story, that believe in you and feel that they belong to your salon. That's how you build great salon culture, you just can't do it alone, not unless you want to stay small and just have a job.

You need some help. You need employees that can take some of the workload and make life easier for you.

Running a salon is too much for one person to do, if you try and do it all on your own you'll end up getting nothing done, burnt out or overwhelmed and that my friend is not a good place to be.

Your role as a modern salon owner is to drive your salon business forward, to attract new clients, to convert them into raving fans and to deliver a remarkable service. And your teams role is to help you deliver an absolutely remarkable service, to all of your clients.

You all have different roles to do in your business, and your staff need to know this. If you try and build this salon on your own you'll be continually nagging your staff over and over again, you'll be forever telling them that they're doing it wrong, you'll be telling them, "This is the way I want it doing".

That is the old way.

I want to show you the new way.

The new way is not all about you, this is not your salon anymore.

Yes, your name's above the door, yes you pay the rent, yes you pay the bills, yes you pay the wages but it's not yours anymore.

If you think about it this way, without staff your salon is nothing, you need them.

Your staff today need to feel like they belong to your salon. That they are part of it.

They are wanting their Kim Kardashian moment and that moment for them while working in your salon is them believing that they belong to this salon.

So in their eyes they feel a part of your salon, a part of the plan, a part of the bigger picture. They actually care enough about your salon like it's their own. This is gold if you can get your staff to this level, because that's when they will work very hard for the salon and not just for themselves. But sadly a lot of salon owners never get this right because they are always telling the staff it's their salon.

Now I don't mean that the staff believe that they own it but they're proud to say they work there. They feel they have a part to play in your salon. They own part of it, in their minds they do anyway.

Remember your role is to **attract** new clients to your business, to **convert** these clients to visit more often and to **deliver** a remarkable service. That's your main role as a salon owner!

Your role is to grow the salon business, and all great business leaders meet with their team and discuss their business growth. Somewhere along the line you're going to have to meet with your team and explain to them what your big dream is for the salon, share your core story with them, and how they are part of this and what part they will play in growing your salon forward.

To do this you are going to have to book out some time in your appointment book and dedicate this important time to your staff and to your salons growth, to get your whole team on board. Like I said, you can't do it alone.

At these team meetings you're going to have to share with them your big picture ideas, because they need to know why it matters.

Sharing the big picture will mean sharing numbers with them, takings, bills, targets, your goals and dreams.

This big picture is going to get them to belong to the salon, and believe in you.

If your dreams are big your staff will help you share the load, they'll pull their weight and your salon will be stronger than ever. If every team member is driving the dream home, the salon will make massive leaps towards it.

The big picture is an absolute must, but so is the stuff that matters, the smaller picture.

They need to know how they fit into the big picture.

And I am going to share with you later on in this chapter how to take your big picture, your yearly goal for the salon and break it down to smaller bites, the smaller picture, your weekly targets so that your staff know what is expected of them. They need to know that their smaller targets are working towards the salons big picture goal.

From big picture goals to small picture targets.

You will need to explain to your team that to achieve the big picture salon goal, they have an important role to play too. That their total yearly takings combined will make the big goal happen. They too have a big picture goal to hit.

And to help them see how well they are heading for their big goal, you will need to meet with them weekly as a team, and quarterly as individuals. You will help them achieve their targets and give them the training needed. You will look for their weak points and make them stronger, in all departments.

To hit targets your team have to believe that they can hit the target you have set for them. Just saying to them, "Your goal for the year is $150,000, now go and achieve it", is too big a number for them to understand how they will hit it. They will not know if they are doing well and are on target or doing poorly and miles away from ever achieving it. You will need to break it down for them, they need it in smaller bites so that they can see at an instant where they are, like weekly check points. That way the smaller picture is very normal in their eyes. Most employees know how much they take each week.

And if they believe that their small weekly target is achievable, they will hit it every single time, then before you know it they'll actually achieve their yearly goal and your salon will hit its big goal.

Your business will grow and your dream will be nearer and nearer to its destination.

So how do we actually start this, what do you need to do?

It's quite simple.

First you need to book some time out in the appointment book and you need to sit down with your team and you'll have to discuss your dreams for the salon.

You're going to talk about all the elements in this book that you want to implement.

The systems that need building.

You're going to talk about the remarkable service, the client journey. You're going to cover all things that can go wrong in the working week and as you and I know, there are multiple things that can go wrong.

You're going to start to build your systems as a team, this way everyone will own the system, and if the staff own it they will make sure that it never breaks.

And if anything goes wrong in the salon, it's the system that's faulted, not the person who made the mistake, we all make mistakes.

If something goes wrong you fix it as a team, you come together to find a solution.

You tweak your systems and you role play the outcome, that's what the team meetings are all about.

In any given week in your salon you might have numerous complaints from clients and your job, your role is to make sure that these complaints get less and less. That means that your salon is getting more and more perfect. The more perfect your salon becomes the more it's able to replicate the perfect service, the wow factor and become the best salon in your town.

But that doesn't happen overnight you've got to sit and observe and watch. When things go wrong in your salon and you see them, you notice staff not rebooking clients, you notice staff not recommending retail products. Instead of diving in there and then which most owners do, because that just causes a big hoo hah in the salon and nobody is going to want to work hard for you, if you're that type of boss. You need to be patient and bring that problem to the team to solve.

Overreacting too soon to staff falling short of their standards has the opposite effect of what you are trying to achieve, What you want is team work, you want the system to be at fault not the staff member, and that means your team will build the systems and keep them strong. Blaming the staff member will just get you exiled from their efforts and it will become a you and them scenario. And that's the last thing you want.

But if you do it properly in a team meeting and bring up the issue, "Hey team I noticed this week that our retail performance wasn't very good, it's dropped off a little. Now we know our systems work because the figures don't lie, so it must mean that we're all probably getting a little bit lazy or complacent. So let's do a role play today and see if we can refresh our consultations in our minds ready for when the clients come in, we'll work on the outcome and the step by steps, that way the retail and the numbers should rise and we'll all get to hit our weekly targets and we'll eventually hit our yearly goals".

That way everybody's responsible for the outcome, and they realise you will be following through if they slack off, they know they're being lazy or they forgot, they're not silly they know that.

This way you're disciplining the system and you do it in the weekly meeting. You bring it to your meeting and you say, "Hey I saw somebody", you don't even need to mention them by name they know who they are. You just need to bring it up that you've noticed it and then the week after at the next team meeting you just follow through and go, "Hey our numbers have gone up, the system's working again awesome, keep it up guys".

Staff need to know that they can relax at work and not be constantly watched and reprimanded for failure, so building systems together and making the systems stronger at each meeting shows the team how important the systems are, how important their contribution is and how important you take growing your salon, booking time out each week to drive this home.

During the meeting remember your can also off load some of your work load, you can talk about social media, what do they think is going to work, share your posts, blogs and videos. Even get them to help you create some of it.

But a team meeting is NOT a bitch fest. This is not you pulling a staff member out and putting them down. This is also NOT a place where staff put other staff members down.

The team meeting is a happy place.

It's about growing your business and I would set that out right at the beginning of your meeting, explaining to them, "Hey guys we're going to start weekly meetings and this is going to be about...", and then explain to them.

Explain to them what a team meeting is not, just like I'm like doing with you now.

It gives them a chance to bring something up that they saw that went wrong, 'some bowls in the basin, some lady who wasn't rebooked back in, a problem with the treatment, ran out of a particular stock item or whatever it may be.'

Your job then, is to remind them that it's the system that they're complaining about and the system is what you and they built, and you and they get to fix it. This is also not a place for you to do a personal attack on them or them on you. It's not a place where you join in and bully staff. It's also not the right time to talk about individual targets and where certain people are individually falling short. You leave that for your quarterly reviews on a one to one basis.

The team meeting planner is about growing your business.

Starting a new year the right way with an extended team meeting will pay dividends with your salons total turnover.

I start my new financial year with an extended team meeting, if this is your first time introducing team meetings to your salon, I would also make this, your very first team meeting an extended one, usually I would book out around two hours.

Your team need to know certain things about your salon to make them feel like they belong, to something bigger than them, their Kim Kardashian moment. You will need to cover this topic in two ways. The bigger picture (the dream of the salon) and the smaller picture (day to day stuff, real world).

The Bigger Picture

Don't forget it's your role to talk about the big picture and how your staff fit into your big picture, how they belong, what their role is in growing the business, because they want to belong remember.

I would get a white board or you could use your mirrors with whiteboard marker or you could just stick paper on the wall and write on that. What matters is showing your team the big picture, which is the salons total takings from last year.

Big Picture - Small Picture

Last Year $500,000 New Goal $650,000				
Amy	Beth	Rich	Tam	Total
$150k	$140k	$160k	$200k	$650k
$2886	$2692	$3,076	$3,846	$12,500

THE LIFESTYLE SALON OWNER

So for example if we took $500,000 last year, I would start with writing $500,000 in the last years section. Then I would explain to the team that we are aiming to increase this year by an extra 30%. I will then explain to them what an increase like this would mean to the salon.

- More hair shows
- More in house training
- Wage increase
- New salon fit out
- Photoshoots
- Hair Expos, etc.

We are going to try to do a 30% increase this coming year so our new salon goal this year is $650,000 so a big increase of course (you can see that I have added it to the picture above).

You'll see underneath on the next line, you'll have individual stylists or therapists names, below that is their individual contribution to last years total takings and yes you share what each staff member did, the full amount, they know what they did, there's no point in hiding it from them.

On the next line down you'll add what their new target is with the 30% increase for the year (take last years total and + 30%).

Your staff might be getting a little worried that the new figure is unachievable right now, and so they should be. It's a big scary amount!

But next you are going to break that bigger picture goal into smaller bites that they can relate to.

The smaller picture

For your staff to actually achieve this goal, you need to be able to break the big picture down into smaller bites, so they can see that the figures

146

you are asking for are achievable, and the best way to do that in their world is break each figure down into weekly amounts.

In the picture you will see the next two lines are dedicated to weekly amounts. Last years weekly takings and now this coming years weekly takings.

You may think 30% is too much to increase in one year, but now you have the knowledge in this book, I think it's worth keeping it at 30%.

They should notice that the difference isn't as big as they first thought as they compare last years figures to this years.

Next you need to explain how you are going to help them achieve this. What part you will play in growing the salon. Remember you are going to **Attract, Convert** and **Deliver** your salon growth.

I would explain that the salon will be having a 5% price rise across the board in May so 5% is going to happen with you doing nothing, nothing at all. You could explain the plans to bring in a new retail line and how that normally lifts takings up by 5%.

You should also share what promotions you are planning for the year and they might have some ideas to help you, you might tell them about the 5 big promotions you're going to put out to fill the quiet days in the salon.

The big campaign you're planning for the 3 quiet months in the year.

What might be happening at Christmas, Easter, Mothers Day and other main holiday events.

What emails you are going to send out to get more clients in.

Letting them know it's a team goal and both you and them have to work hard to achieve it, you both have different roles but with the same big picture goal, will help them understand the need to lift their game.

You will show them, if they're not at full capacity, how many more clients they need to hit this new weekly target, or how much higher the average spend needs to be to achieve the new target.

This is also a great time to explain 'what's in it for them' if they hit their new weekly targets, I would share what new bonuses they're going to get, what commissions they're going to get, what great things are going to happen to the salon as a result of them hitting their targets.

This hopefully will get them excited for the year ahead.

At this stage I will usually play a game with them now to find their personal goals for the year.

My aim is, if they hit their salon targets, I will help them achieve their personal goals.

"If we achieve the salon big picture goal, there will be enough money in the pot to help you achieve your goals", maybe they want a new car and we're going to show them that if they hit this they'll earn enough commission to buy a new car or to get married or to have a holiday or to buy a house.

The secret to any salon success is team work.

Getting the team to believe in your dream, your core story, getting the team to believe it's actually achievable.

The big picture is achievable, the smaller picture is achievable.

Throughout this book, I have been explaining that your clients and your staff need to feel like they belong. This big picture stuff is how you get your staff to believe that they belong, remember I said they feel like it's their salon, they are part of it, they need something bigger than them? Well, this is their Kim Kardashian moment. This is where they sit with their friends in a coffee shop and tell them all about what they have achieved at your salon.

This big picture stuff is powerful.

I would like to share a story about my big picture, in my salon.

My big picture was a 30% increase from last years taking of $550,000 to a goal of $715,000

I did exactly what I outlined above, big picture - small picture, extended meeting and got all the staff on board.

I also, as an added bonus, decided to reward my team with a BIG audacious reward.

The reward was a trip around the world for two staff members, to learn new cut and colour techniques from the worlds best. They would fly into London and Paris, and as my salon is in Sydney Australia that's a big reward.

So the big picture reward was set. But they needed the small picture to keep them motivated on a weekly basis.

The small picture of this reward was, for every week that they hit their weekly target they could put a token in a jam jar. Simple!

So I gave every team member 48 marbles each, every staff member had a different colour, and if they hit their weekly targets they could place 1 marble into the jar.

At the end of the year I would pull out 2 marbles of different colours and

THE LIFESTYLE SALON OWNER

they would be the winning team members that would win the round the world trip. They were even allowed to take their partners too.

Everyone had 48 chances to put all their marbles in the jar, even the apprentices had a target also.

This was very effective because even if you have a lot less marbles than other team members, you are still in with the running, anything can happen.

This particular year almost every staff member hit their weekly goals.

And we smashed our big picture goal too, smashed it out of the park.

Your team meetings are important and time invested in them is invaluable in the growth of your salon business. You get to share your teams wins throughout the week, and keep your systems strong.

Without a team meeting it's hard to keep all your team on the same page, cracks will appear in your systems and your staff will start to believe that the big picture is unachievable.

Remember they need that Kim Kardashian moment.

If you don't supply it, they'll look elsewhere for it.

I could never have had the success that my salon gave me without team meetings.

Go book that meeting right now.

CASE STUDY

My doubts were I really can't afford this at the moment

But then I felt if you continue what you are doing you will continue to get the same results and we needed a kick up the bum and needed guidance and told where to start

I am loving the course but. It is intense there is so much to do it didn't go down well with my staff trying to change so many things all at once they felt I was giving them more work to do

Now just doing 1 or 2 things a week trying to make it fun as well upping personal daily figures by $50 they are pleased when they beat their own targets

All staff encouraged to make an advert for Facebook doing research on products and using pink slip principles so they are getting in depth knowledge of products!!

A win getting a 2 week in apprentice to help write up some systems and procedures it works

The initial salon questionnaire I filled in had some obvious questions we didn't have in place like do we have a price list in windows? No we didn't haven't for a couple of years as they have disappeared when the door opens and been blown away

Now we do have price list in our 3 salon windows and have noticed how many people do look at it

That was so simple and an obvious mistake of ours

We did a Facebook ad for blondes and said we are blonde experts

We are getting new clients that want to be blonde !!

We now ask new clients how they found us and surprisingly google so we realise we need to spend money on website more than Facebook

I am tracking figures more and am more aware of client numbers and average spend each week

Also Xmas packs from reps which we buy without fail each year now I realise we are not making much profit just giving them a huge order and getting a massive invoice to pay we are going to be smarter this year

Doing this course has given me the motivation to want change and improve the business or get out and I don't want that yet when things are tough and you are despairing you need to know there is something else you can do even if it as simple as getting the price list in the window

Sharon Johnson, The Salon Hair Design, Perth, Western Australia

Conclusion

I'm sure that right now, if you're anything like me you're probably feeling pumped, excited, overwhelmed and raring to go, and I totally understand that. The strategies I've laid out here in this book took me over 10 years to discover from dozens of different mentors, books, seminars and a whole lot of trial and error.

I wish I'd had something like this when I got started. I hope that instead of feeling overwhelmed, you'll realise that this is actually a huge shortcut.

I only shared in these pages those things that have been proven to work in my own salons and of salon owners in my coaching program, the 'Lifestyle Salon System'.

You can have faith, knowing that you're not implementing stuff that has not been proven to work in today's salon world.

I hope that reading this book has been a great investment of your time.

I also invite you to join our private Facebook group, 'The Lifestyle Salon Owner' full of salon owners just like yourself. https://www. facebook.com/groups/The LifestyleSalonOwners/

I spend a lot of time in there, helping salon owners grow their businesses.

We started this book by talking about a **Lifestyle Salon System**.

I said there were 3 things that you needed to do.

You need to **attract**, you need to **convert**, and you need to **deliver**.

I have talked about the only 3 ways to grow your salon business:

Attract - Get more bums on seats, more clients in your salon.

Convert - Get the bums on seats to visit you more often, to get your clients to come and visit you more regularly.

Deliver - Get bums on seats to spend more with you, to increase your clients average bill.

In **chapter 1** I talked about moving away from doing specials and discounts and moving towards your salon being the authority in town and how everybody wants to go to the expert person in town.

How to figure out how your clients problems can be converted into your marketing campaigns, so that your clients know who your salon is for.

In **chapter 2** I talked about converting these prospective clients, once they hear about you, and how not many salon owners will follow through and build this intangible system to make a connection, to guide them to your website to expel the bargain chasers and to convert them to come to your salon so that when they come they're raving fans and will pay whatever it takes to get their problem fixed.

You can even convert your current clients to visit you more often and to actually fill your quiet staff members on your quietest days.

In **chapter 3** I talked about how to deliver a remarkable service, how your customer service being average is not good enough any more and how your salon is being judged by everything and anyone that your clients do business with, not just other hair salons. Also how delivering a remarkable service raises your clients average bill and stops you becoming the main drawcard and that now the salon becomes the destination.

These 3 main chapters work solely on the only 3 ways to grow any business, your business:

To **attract** more clients to your salon.

To **convert** them to come more regularly.

To **deliver** a remarkable service so that your average bill goes up and they spend more with you.

You would have also learnt that there are 3 types of salon owners and by now you should know which owner you are.

If you're in the **Start Up Zone** how the passion will take you from that zone into the **War Zone**, quite naturally.

If you're in the **War Zone** how your passion alone will not be able to take you out of this zone and how the **War Zone** salon owner needs to have certain systems in place, certain strategies to get them out of the **War Zone** and take them into the **Lifestyle Zone**.

The **Lifestyle Salon System** is the key, it's your pathway from being stuck in the **War Zone** to bumping yourself up quickly and becoming a **lifestyle** salon owner.

We broke down the 9 strategies, the 9 projects that turn your salon into a lifestyle salon business.

You can do the same too. What I am going to do next is walk you through the **Lifestyle Salon System** plan that we use with our **Lifestyle Salon System** clients.

It will help you take everything you've learned so far and apply it into your world quickly.

Here are things you need to know before we get started.

I wanted to offer all of my readers a really special offer.

If you're like me when you buy a book and you read it, you're super keen to actually get going as quickly as possible, but you come to a full stop very quickly because you get stuck in overwhelm.

You see my online programs are specifically designed to take you from the **War Zone** to the **Lifestyle Zone** as quickly as possible.

I've done so much of the hard work for you that it is easy to implement, even with very little time.

All of what I have done is proven to work in salons around the world.

Salons like yours.

I've used them in my own salons and I've taught them in my courses for years.

It's called the **Lifestyle Salon System**.

If you want to get your hands on a great workshop and start growing your salon enabling you to get clients and make money fast without having to think too hard, I have a special workshop just for you. Click link below to access it.

https://isaloncoaching.lpages.co/workshop-lifeststyle/

CASE STUDY

WHY ME WHY NOW

After initially being in business for 7 years I decided I needed a coach, the salon was in the red, lots of overdue bills and couldn't pay things on time.

We started out very busy and the salon had early success but then I spent most days putting out fires. The salon grew really fast, I took on more staff but I didn't have any systems in place. Systems to track the growth, or systems at all for that matter. Having taken time off to have my kids I realised that when I wasn't in the salon, because there weren't any systems in place the day to day basics that needed to get done, didn't happen. I had a manager but she had no direction when I wasn't there. I realised that I needed someone to hold me accountable and help me put systems in place.

WHY ME

I have been to a few seminars that talked about marketing and I thought that maybe that was why the salon wasn't making enough money, because I wasn't marketing properly. So I did what most people do, I started Googling things and I joined a few hairdressing specific groups on FB and you Richard McCabe kept popping up. So I followed Richard for a while, watched some of your videos and it seemed very real, because you were once a hairdresser, you had had salons of your own. I was being stalked by other coaches and marketers all claiming to be able to help me, but none of them seemed specific to our industry. From the time I made that first phone call with Richard it felt like I was talking to someone I'd know for 20 years. It was really easy; he was really natural and personable.

WHAT WOULD IT HAVE BEEN LIKE IF WE HADN'T CONNECTED

It became harder after having kids to be able to spend the amount of time we needed to spend on the floor and there was no one working the behind the scenes stuff. We (my sister and I) were at a stage where we were having to put our own money in to the salon to pay the bills. We had done that for a year to keep the business afloat but obviously you can't do that forever. We would have crashed if we continued like that, we weren't making any profit. We were in the red.

I have come to the realisation since having a coach that the salon earns more money, the less time I work on the floor, so making sure I take the time out to work on the business side of things and having those systems in place, and having a team that believes in the systems has been the biggest thing for me because now if I'm not in the salon, the salon does operate the same as if I am there

HOW HAS OUR 12 MONTHS TOGETHER GONE FOR YOU

Financially the salon turned around really quickly once I made some big decisions. I'm sure other people think after 12 months they know everything now and they don't need a coach anymore, but for me I think the cost is a small price to pay to keep me accountable and to keep educating myself. I no longer want to go out and do a hair workshop or a colour workshop I want to be able to pay for my staff to do those. I feel that the cost of a coach is just my education, for me to continually grow, and hopefully you as the coach are continually learning new things and that then I get the benefit of that.

WHAT WOULD YOU SUGGEST TO ANYONE THINKING OF GETTING A COACH

I can't believe I didn't get a coach sooner. I just jumped into owning a business, I thought I knew what I was doing but clearly I didn't.

CONCLUSION

Connecting with Richard was the best thing I could have done. Having someone who knows the systems and helps to implement them is invaluable. I would recommend it any one.

Kristy, Koto Hair, VIC, Australia

Let's Make A Plan For Action

There are two kinds of people that set plans, one will set big goals, will plan it down in fine detail and doesn't vary far from the plan itself. They know their numbers, they know what needs to get done and they find it easy to make it happen.

BTW if that's you, you can just run with what you have learnt in this book and you'll know exactly what you need to do next.

But if you're the second one, like me, and many other salon owners, I don't know where to start first, how to begin, what to start with, but I am so pumped to get going, I'll end up doing everything like a bull in a china shop until it all becomes too difficult and messy that I'll stop and my dream to get my salon into the Lifestyle Zone, live a great lifestyle will be just that, a dream.

Then this last part of the book has been written just for you.

My coach 'Taki Moore' showed me how to do this in his book and it action planned my success, so I want to share this with you also.

You can create a simple and easy plan, 'a get stuff done plan' which is created for the creative mind, just the type that a salon owner will love. The 'get stuff done plan' isn't a typical business plan as you know it ; it's not full of what-ifs, SWOT analyses, or risk assessments. It's a very practical what needs to get done this week sort of plan. It's a how do I get bums on seats sort of plan. How do I grow your salon and make money sort of plan?

The 'get stuff done plan' is just the right amount of your big picture vision mixed with what needs to get done today to make it happen. Instead of setting a long-winded plan in stone forever, we want a simple 'get stuff done' plan that gives you direction and tells you exactly what you need to do today, right now, this minute.

When I first set my salon goal, I spent weeks planning out this huge goal and plan, with numbers and pictures and writing. Within 2 months the plan was obsolete, I lost a staff member and the numbers all became irrelevant. So I used this simple 'get stuff done plan'

In my Lifestyle Salon Systems we go deep with this plan, we call it a sprint. Where we sprint through 30 days to achieve a project and 'get stuff done'

We try and think about big picture stuff (we all need to know where we are going, so we stay on track) and what steps we need to make to get there (small projects, that keep us on track) and what needs to be done today (where do we start, and how to get there).

In a moment, we're going to create a 'get stuff done plan' that covers your big picture (your dream).

Big Picture Stuff

Where do you want your salon to be in three years time?
What are your 12 month goals?
What are your projects for the next three months?
What do you need to work on today?

You can just grab a blank sheet of paper and divide it into four quadrants.

We're going to start up in the top left corner, write vision-3 years.

Where do you want to be in three years' time?
What do you want your salon business to look like in three years?
How do you want things to be different?

How do you want your takings, your personal income to be different?

Write that down in the top left box.

Start writing now.

Just bullet points, first things that comes to mind.

Write them down.

How do you want your staff to be different?

What about your services and retail?

How do you want your life to be different?

How do you want your reputation in your town to be different?

How do you want to be known by your clients, in the industry, by your peers? What do your weeks look like? Are you still working 5 days, are you off the floor?

12 months

Let's look at the top, right-hand side. We've thought about the big three year goal and vision, and how you want your salon to look and your life to be, now let's bring it down a little bit closer to home.

PLAN FOR ACTION

We're thinking about 12 months, and goals. Here's what comes next. We've just painted a picture; we've created a vision for our next three years. What we're going to do next is look at taking steps to achieve your 3-year goal.

I believe a 30% increase is a good place to start.

So your 12 month goal starting point should be where your takings are now and add a 30% increase to them (hopefully doing that every year will make you reach or surpass your 3 year plan)

Now, most people, when they're breaking down their goals, they just assume that everything's going to pan out. Have you ever noticed that things don't work out like that? You have to be ready to bob and weave sometimes, to re focus where you are and how you get back on track, the 'get stuff done plan' is perfect for this.

In the top right box, write down your takings goals for the 12 months, where you need to be in a year? Look at everything you've got in the top left box (3 year plan) and write down the one-year version of it in the right hand box. Make each one very tactical, very measurable. The question is, "How much, by when?" The when's decided, it's one year, so you just have to decide how much. You want to look at your list in a year's time and check each box.

Did I achieve that, or didn't I?

90 days

Now we're going to zoom down to what needs to get done, to the bottom left box.

PLAN fOR AcTIoN

We're not thinking about the three year, or the 12 month goals.

Your new time frame is 90 days.

I think 90 days is a great milestone to take stock and see if you are on the right track to reaching your 12 month goal.

I also think that doing one project well, extremely well, it will take massive steps to taking your salon to the **Lifestyle Zone.**

Each chapter in the book is going to be a project for you to work on.

You will want to work fast and hard to master the projects so they don't drag on, and you and your staff don't get bored.

You should be aiming for one project a month.

I would work hard for 90 days and then take a breather for the next 30 days. So I don't burn out. Work hard then rest. Then start all over again.

But right now we're not thinking about vision or goals; we're thinking about projects, stuff that needs to get done on a weekly basis so in 12 months you have actually achieved your goal. Goals don't just happen; so action is needed and projects will give you the 'what' needs to get done to achieve this.

The question is this: "If you know where you want to be in 12 months time, what are the three projects you need to get done in the next 90 days to be completely on track?"

Okay, we're down to the last step.

Here's what you do.

Now, if you've got some Post-it notes handy, that would be great if not go and buy some. I like to be creative here and see things getting done.

Take 3 post it notes and write down your 3 projects you are going to do first, you can do any project (chapters), in any order you wish. I would advise doing the ones that your salon needs first, and stick them in the 90 day box, one on top of the other.

Now to complete your project in 30 days time you need to start on something right now, today. Your new timeframe is one week, and we're talking about the specific actions you need to make your projects complete.

The question you need to be thinking about right now is, "If those are my 30-day projects, what three actions do I need to take this week to help me get closer to completing it?"

Next 7 days

So what are the one, two, three actions you need to take in the next seven days to move yourself forward?

And I suggest making one of them really easy, something you can do in less than two minutes, anything super simple that gets you moving forward.

When you complete your three actions each week, you're on track with your 90-day projects.

If you complete your 90-day projects, you'll be on track with your 12-month goals.

The Lifestyle Salon System - Plan for Action

If you hit your 12-month goals, you'll be completely on track for your three-year vision.

Focus on your three actions for this week, and the rest will take care of itself.

This is what we do with every client in our Lifestyle Salon Systems, every month we start a new 30 day project, if you would like more help on your 30 day project and feel that you would like us to help you please feel free to email me at richard@isaloncoaching.com

If you're serious about growing your salon, we should talk about the Lifestyle Salon Courses.

The first is Foundational Salon System, If you are a smaller salon that's in their Start Up stage or stuck in the War Zone, with limited turnover this program is a must for you. It's been built especially with you in mind and will not put any more financial burden on you. This course will make your salon foundations strong and grow your business to a level where you can escape the War Zone. Just email me at richard@ isaloncoaching.com with the subject line '**Foundational Salon System**' and I'll send you all the information you need to get started straight away.

If you want to grow your salon business to another level, and your salon is already established, but you just want to work less and earn more, to build a lifestyle salon, then the **Lifestyle Salon Systems** is the course for you.

Just email: richard@isaloncoaching.com with the subject line '**Lifestyle Salon Systems**' and I will contact you so we can have a quick chat to determine if we can help you or not.

At the time of writing this book Richard McCabe is the fastest growing Lifestyle salon Coach in Australia.

He coaches well over 100 salon owners every week on how to implement these simple strategies outlined in this book, to grow their salons from the **War Zone** into the **Lifestyle Zone**. Because these strategies work and clients love the results they get, they refer him to all of their friends.

He has personally changed hundreds of salon owners lives as they now work less in their businesses and earn more. More Freedom, More Money, More Purpose! Because that's what we all want don't we?

The **Lifestyle Salon Systems** is the only salon only program that is built on the 3 main principles of growing any business, because anything else to learn would just be a waste of time and effort.

Attract new clients to your salon

Convert them to visit your salon more often

Deliver a remarkable service to them so they spend more and increase your salons average bill.

These 9 simple strategies will transform your salon from the **War Zone** to the **Lifestyle** you deserve, because each strategy will lay down the foundations to grow your business the right way, the only way a business can increase its takings.

These strategies are working in salons around the world and getting salon owners just like you explosive results because they have been proven to work in the real world and have been adapted to todays modern salon, with todays savvy clients.

Every strategy in this book is all about 'doing' and not learning, because it's not about learning, learning does NOT get you results 'doing' does.

Your salon needs to master each and every one of these 9 strategies to become a Lifestyle Salon. Because you can have faith, knowing that you're not implementing stuff that has not been proven in the salon world.

Below are just a few testimonials of clients that I am working with right now and their results. You will have also seen many case studies in this book from real clients of mine and their results too.

You can check out what other salon owners have said about us here:

https://lifestylesaloncoach.com/salon-owners-say-us/

Because I want to be able to help you to be the best you can, and that means to decide if this course is suitable for you, and also if we are going to be good to work together. If we are not, I will surely direct you to the right place that I feel will help you the most.

What to do now?

If you want to go deeper with the 9 strategies, learn quicker and get faster results, then I can help you become the best of the best in your town.

Throughout this book, I've talked a lot about the 3 ways to grow your salon business, and that's great. It's important! What's going to make the difference to you and your salons growth is implementation. It all comes down to you.

Are you ready to take your salon to new and bigger heights?

I'd love to meet you sometime at a live workshop, in my Facebook group or in a program.

Please, spread the word about this book and the website, so more salon owners can become free of the **War Zone**.

Share with your friends: www.isaloncoaching.com

If there's anything I can ever do, please let me know.

Thanks so much for being part of my world, for spending this time with me and I wish you every success for the future.

With that said, I encourage you to master the skills in this book, and I'd love to know how you are getting on.

Please let's not be strangers, and let's grow your salon together. Email: richard@isaloncoaching.com anytime.

Remember how to eat an elephant, one bit at a time.

Richard McCabe

Lifestyle Salon Coach

PS: Remember, you're just one client away…

Click here for your free copy of 'How A Salon Coach Is Good For Your Wealth'

https://lifestylesaloncoach.com/wpcontent/uploads/2017/07/Owning-A-Salon-Is-Good-For-Your-Wealth.pdf

Remember I'm here for you.

My mission is to help 1,000 hair salon owners get out of the WAR ZONE, let's do this together

If you'd like a FREE business check up click on the link below and I will personally evaluate your business for you:

https://lifestylesaloncoach.com/lifestyle-salon-business-check/

Just email: richard@isaloncoaching.com with the subject line 'Mission War Zone' and I will send you some great videos of mine to watch.

Printed in Great Britain
by Amazon